Haynes

Build your own
Computer

3rd Edition

© Haynes Publishing 2005
First published 2003
Reprinted 2004 (twice)
Second edition published 2005
Reprinted 2006
Third edition published 2007

Published by: Haynes Publishing
Sparkford, Yeovil, Somerset BA22 7JJ, UK
Tel: 01963 442030 Fax: 01963 440001
Int. tel: +44 1963 442030 Fax: +44 1963 440001
E-mail: sales@haynes.co.uk
Website: www.haynes.co.uk

British Library Cataloguing in Publication Data:
A catalogue record for this book is available from the British Library

ISBN 978 1 84425 457 6

Printed in Britain by J. H. Haynes & Co. Ltd., Sparkford

Haynes

Build your own Computer

3rd Edition

Contents

Introduction   **6**

 Planning the 'perfect' PC   **8**
Four good reasons to build your own computer   10
How to shop   12
Where to shop   14
Hard and soft options   16

 Choosing your hardware   **20**
Motherboard   22
Processor   34
Memory   39
Case   45
Power supply unit   48
Hard disk drive   51
Sound card   56
Video card   59
Optical drives   63
Other possibilities   67
The perfect PC   72

 Putting together a dual-core PC   **76**
All set?   78
Installing the processor and heatsink   80
Installing RAM   86
Installing the motherboard   88
Installing the power supply unit   94
Installing the DVD drive, card reader
  and hard disk   96
Installing the video card   102

Assembling an Athlon SFF PC   **104**
Upfront preparation   106
Fleshing out the barebones   108
Installing the drives   114
Installing the video and expansion cards   118

Final touches   **120**
Connecting a monitor and switching on   122
Essential system settings   124
Installing Windows Vista   128
Installing a sound card   135
Digital audio extraction   137
Loose ends   138
Free software   140
Troubleshooting   146

Appendices   **150**
Appendix 1 – Silence is golden ... well,
copper and aluminium   152
Appendix 2 – That's entertainment:
  making a media centre PC   154
Appendix 3 – Beep and error codes   158
Appendix 4 – Further resources   163
Appendix 5 – Abbreviations and acronyms   165

Index   **166**

Acknowledgements   **168**

Introduction

Welcome to this fully updated and revised guide to building your own PC. There have been some big changes in the world of PCs since the first and second editions of this book were published – there's a brand new version of Windows, Windows Vista, and the familiar Pentium processor has been superseded by Core Duo chips – so we've taken this opportunity to cover the very latest processors, memory, interfaces and more.

We've brought this book bang up to date, but of course the important things remain the same. We'll focus squarely on the practical essentials – what to get, where to get it at the best price and how to put it all together – and we'll keep jargon to an absolute minimum. We'll also cover two kinds of PC project: a powerful and enormously upgradeable PC that will last you for years and years, and a tiny PC that's perfect for putting in your front room.

Why do I want to build my own computer?

That's a very good question. After all, few of us build our own houses or our own cars, so why on earth should you build your own computer when you can just buy one from a shop? There are several really good reasons and the most important one is this: If building a car was as easy and as flexible as building a computer, you'd be driving a car that looked like an Aston Martin, handled like a Porsche, had the same luggage space as a Saab Estate, was as quiet as a Lexus and used less petrol than a Toyota Prius.

Building your own computer is the only way to get a perfect PC. So what makes a PC perfect? There are four key criteria. It should fit your needs exactly; it should be flexible; it should be easily expandable; and it should be affordable. Let's look at each of those criteria in more detail.

The perfect PC fits your needs exactly When you buy a ready-made PC, it's likely to be a good all-rounder, and while there's nothing wrong with that it does mean it probably won't be perfect for the things you actually want it to do. While most manufacturers enable you to change various options – so you can specify a slightly bigger hard disk, say, or a slightly better graphics card – the available options are usually fairly limited. For example, manufacturers typically offer two or three different graphics cards on a particular PC, but there are hundreds of such cards out there. It's entirely possible that the right one for you isn't available from that particular manufacturer – or that if the right one is available, the right hard disk isn't, or it doesn't come with the particular processor you'd prefer, or you don't like the look of the PC's case. And so on.

When you build your own PC you don't have to compromise, so if you want a really quick PC that can happily handle video editing, has all the necessary connectors for your cameras and camcorder and doesn't sound like a jumbo jet when you use it

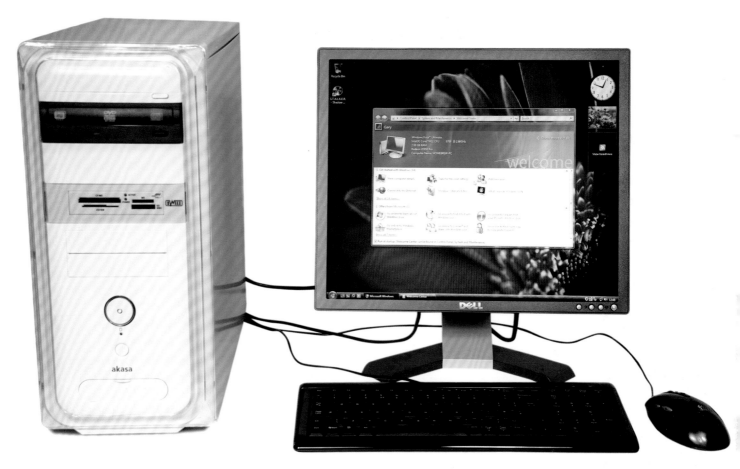

then that's what you build. Alternatively, you might want a cheap and cheerful PC that doesn't take up much room, doesn't cost the earth and doesn't bankrupt you when the electricity bill arrives. Once again, if you want it you can build it.

The perfect PC is flexible The days when PCs were used only for dull work things are long gone, and today's PCs should be able to handle anything you can throw at them – managing your digital photos, editing your home movies, playing games, burning DVDs and so on. More importantly, a perfect PC should be able to handle anything you throw at it in the future too, so for example a PC that's struggling with today's games won't be able to handle the latest releases in a year or two. When you build your own PC you can make sure it's not only powerful enough for what you want to do today, but for what you want to do tomorrow too.

The perfect PC is expandable It's impossible to predict what you might want to do in the future. You might not fancy video editing now, but in a year's time you might be making home movies of the kids or even making your own spy thrillers in the shed – at which point you discover that your graphics card really isn't up to the job. Or you might decide to digitise your record collection and store all your albums in MP3 format – and within weeks, your hard disk is positively packed. With an expandable PC, both

problems are easy to solve. In the first scenario, you'd simply pop in a new graphics card and, in the second, you'd add another hard disk. Easy.

The trick to expandability is planning. If you make sure the PC you build today sticks to established industry standards and avoids technologies that are already heading into history, you'll be able to upgrade it easily and affordably for many years to come.

The perfect PC is affordable Anyone can pop into a shop and spend £1,000 on a 'ready for anything' computer, but how many of its features will you actually use? Shops and websites are big fans of bundled hardware and software, but in many cases you'll find that for every goodie you get, a corner has probably been cut somewhere – so the PC has a free printer, but it really needs more memory; it comes with a giant monitor, but it'd run much faster with a slightly smaller screen and a more powerful video card; it comes with lots of software, but you're getting the frankly rubbish Home Basic edition of Windows Vista instead of the all-singing, all-dancing Home Premium or Ultimate editions.

When you buy a PC, the manufacturer decides what you need to pay and what you'll get for your money. When you build your own, you choose not only what goes into your PC, but also how much you're willing to pay for it. Does that sound like your sort of system? Then read on.

PART  # Planning the 'perfect' PC

Four good reasons to build your own computer   10
How to shop   12
Where to shop   14
Hard and soft options   16

By doing all the donkey work yourself, you might justly
assume that you can build a new computer for less than
you'd pay in the shops. The truth may surprise you: you
probably can't. But before you return this manual to the
bookstore in a fit of pique, consider both the reasons
why ... and the reasons why it doesn't matter.

PART 1

Four good reasons to build your own computer

While it's true that you can buy precisely the same components from a retail outlet as an OEM (see p.12) can source direct from the manufacturer, you pay a considerable premium. It's not a level playing field, with the result that it can cost rather more to build your own system than to buy an off-the-peg identikit computer. And yet there are four good reasons why this really doesn't matter. These, indeed, are the reasons why we wrote this manual.

UNBEATABLE OFFER

Athlon XP 5000+++ Processor!
Massive 256MB DDR SD-RAM
Super-Big 60GB Hard Disk (5,400rpm)
Combo 52/ 48/12/6/2/1 x CD-
R/RW/DVD+R/+RW

2 x USB Ports + Modem!   Integrated Audio!!!!
15-inch TFT Monitor!!   Six Speakers!!!!!
Integrated Graphics!!!   £££s free software!!!!!!

CALL NOW 0800 245959

Bargain of the century or a duff deal in disguise? If you've ever browsed the adverts and waded through specs, you'll know just how confusing buying a computer can be. So don't do it. Build one instead.

1. Satisfaction

Building your own computer is an immensely satisfying project. You're about to construct something from scratch that few people, even those who use them day in and day out, perhaps even you yourself, really understand. If that's not worth a pat on the back and a cup of kudos, we don't know what is.

2. Knowledge

To build a computer, you have to understand how everything fits together and be able sort out the important specifications from the marketing hype. When an advert proudly proclaims 'Blazing Pentium 4 3GHz+++ power!!!', and you can't believe the price, you can be sure that corners have been cut somewhere. But where, exactly? The answer is usually buried deep within the detailed specifications or hidden altogether: integrated graphics without an expansion slot for future upgrades, perhaps, or a cheap and nasty sound card, or insufficient memory. Read this manual in full and you'll know precisely where to look; build your own computer and you'll never be sold short again. The practical experience you'll gain in a DIY project of this nature is all you'll ever need to tackle computers with confidence for years to come.

3. Save money

Yes, despite what we said above, you can build a new PC on the cheap. The problem computer manufacturers and retailers alike face is one of having to be seen to offer the very latest kit at all times and at all cost – and that cost is borne by you, the consumer. But you don't necessarily need the latest kit, so why pay over the odds for PC performance that you'll never exploit? The key is compromising where you can and not where you shouldn't. By opting for a slightly slower processor and upping the ante elsewhere, you can make a PC that will outperform its shop-bought equivalent in every area – and save you money into the bargain.

4. It's the only PC you'll ever need

A bold claim indeed but one we feel confident in making. There are two really important points about building your own computer: you get to design it from the ground up to do precisely what you want it to do and, provided you start from a sound base, you can expand, upgrade, re-equip and otherwise enhance your computer more or less forever. Flexibility is the key.

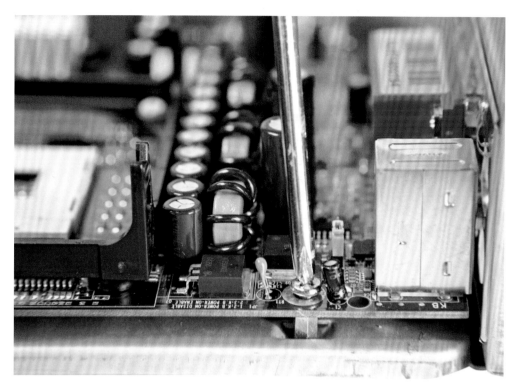

The ultimate upgrade: replacing an outmoded – or broken – motherboard. But rather that, surely, than shelling out on a whole new system.

Pull the other one

But surely my computer will be out of date in a year anyway, you cry? Well, let's just examine that notion for a moment. Bits of it may no longer meet your changing needs, that is true, but the point is that you can upgrade your hardware to suit. It's never possible to predict changes in technology with absolute certainty but we can at least say that the SATA and PCI Express interfaces are here now and here to stay (more of which anon). All you have to do is choose a motherboard that supports the very latest technology – even if you don't actually *need* this technology right away – to guarantee a measure of future-proofing. An upgrade down the line is always going to be much, much cheaper than the cost of a new system so spending a few extra pounds now on a state-of-the-art motherboard has to be worthwhile.

Or let's imagine that a drive gives up the ghost somewhere down the line. No matter: a hardware failure is a temporary inconvenience, not a reason to replace your PC. Because you built the system in the first place, you'll know just how to fix it.

Even if one day you have to replace the motherboard in order to acquire new interfaces, you can probably reuse the case, power supply, some expansion cards and drives, plus the keyboard, mouse, monitor and everything else. The notion that computers must be replaced every two or three years to keep pace with advancing technology may fuel the industry and keep the tills ringing, but it's largely a marketing myth. Are you really inclined to treat something that costs between £500 and £1,500 as a mere 'commodity', a disposable mod con with a useful lifespan measured in months?

The downside?

Well … you will have to buy your operating system and application software separately instead of getting it bundled with a new system. This means extra expense. Then again, the software thrown in with new computers isn't really free; the cost is merely hidden within the system price and you could end up paying unwittingly for several programs that you don't really want and would never dream of purchasing separately.

Nor do you get an all-encompassing service contract, warranty or technical support when you build your own PC. But would you rather do without your computer for a week or more while it's away getting repaired – or fix it yourself in an hour? Besides, every component you buy will come with its own full warranty.

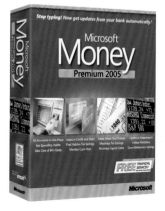

New systems generally come with Windows and a few applications – some of them even useful – pre-installed. When you build your own PC, remember to factor in the cost of new software.

PART  How to shop

Most PCs are constructed with components that are readily available on the open market. There's no great secret to it, really: all you need is a case, a power supply, a motherboard and a bunch of expansion cards and drives. True, some major-league manufacturers use proprietary parts that bind you to them for the lifetime of the computer – i.e. there's no other way to get spares and upgrades – but we're not concerned with such nonsense here.

An OEM would scoff at pretty packaging but there's a lot to be said for a retail product that gives you everything you need in the box. A motherboard, for instance, should include hard and floppy drive cables, a heatsink retention frame, installation screws, an I/O shield, chipset drivers, a manual and a warranty.

OEM vs retail

An OEM is a company that builds and sells computer systems with parts sourced from other companies. With access to the same parts, you can put together a system just as easily as any mass manufacturer. Indeed, should you wish to, you could put together the very same system. But better still, you can build the perfect PC for you: not necessarily the fastest computer on the block or the cheapest, but one that's custom-built to serve your needs both now and in the future.

There's really only one difference between components used by industry and those sold to consumers, and that's in the packaging. Consumer products sport fancy boxes and fancier price tags and fill the shelves of superstores. You get everything you need in the box, including screws, cables, driver software and possibly an application or two. But an OEM has no need for frills and fripperies; rather, it buys bare components in bulk. A 'boxed' or 'retail' or 'consumer' (the terms mean the same thing in this context) Pentium or Athlon processor comes with a compatible heatsink and an instruction manual. The OEM buys exactly the same processor in trays of 1,000 with no extras whatsoever. Guess who pays less?

You, the intrepid system builder, are not supposed to be able to get your hands on OEM stock, but it does filter its way through specialist shops, direct vendors and computer fairs. So long as you're prepared to obtain your own cables, fittings, drivers and sundry other bits and bobs, an OEM component is usually a very good buy indeed. OEM software is worth seeking out, too: OEM versions of Windows and Microsoft Office are much, much cheaper than their retail equivalents. You don't get manuals – or any technical support whatsoever – but you'll save a stack of money.

New vs old

You can buy computer components from many different sources. The first obvious distinction is between new and old, about which we need say little. A used expansion card, drive, power

When a power supply unit's air vents looks like this, you can be sure it has been round the block a few times. Nothing a blast of compressed air won't clear, of course, but you have to wonder how much life it has left.

supply or even motherboard may well perform absolutely perfectly for years to come, or it may already be five minutes removed from hardware heaven. Truth is, it's usually impossible to tell just by looking. Buyer beware – big time.

By their very nature, used components are not cutting-edge. This is absolutely fine: you might, for instance, want to build a basic workstation for web surfing, email, word processing and perhaps a little image editing and printing. Such a system requires only a relatively modest specification – even a Pentium II-based machine will be fine – and it would be wasteful and pointless to build-in surround sound and 3D graphics.

However, there are two important caveats. First, your computer will not be particularly amenable to future upgrades. Should it need a serious performance boost to keep pace with your changing habits, you won't be able to swap the processor for a Core 2 Duo, add an extra slice of fast DDR-RAM or slot in a PCI Express graphics card for gaming. You might not even be able to add a larger hard disk drive, as older BIOS programs don't always recognise today's massive disks. Windows has become more hungry over time, too, so you might be stuck with an older, unsupported operating system: Windows XP won't run on less than a 233MHz processor (and, believe us, even that's very optimistic) and Windows Vista is hungrier still: Home Basic needs a 1GHz processor with 512MB of RAM, and the Premium and Ultimate editions need 1GB of RAM.

Now, all of this is fine so long as you know what you're getting into. Bottom line: today's bargain-basement project is unlikely to serve you well if you need a supercomputer tomorrow.

Also, and this might rather pain you, you can almost certainly pick up a complete, well-worn but perfectly serviceable second-hand computer system for much less than the cost of building one from scratch. Check the small ads, use an online auction site such as eBay, try a reconditioned computer specialist such as Morgan or just ask around. Chances are you can pick one up for a song, perhaps sold without a monitor or extras like the keyboard and mouse. End result? A basic but functional and upgradeable-to-a-degree computer that's worth several times the price of its parts.

And so ...

In short, when building rather than buying a computer, we believe it makes sense to adopt the very latest technology in several key interrelated areas, notably the motherboard, processor and memory. With up-to-date components at the heart of your system, a degree of future-proofing is guaranteed. Everything else, from the mouse to the monitor, from the scanner to the sound card, can be a compromise.

eBaY.co.uk The World's Online Marketplace	HP Vectra VEi8 P3-500 128mg Sony 17" Trintron	£195.00	Buy It Now
	DELL PIII-450 128MB 6.4GB CD SND **£104.00**	£104.00	Buy It Now
	COMPAQ PIII-500 INTERNET READY +15" MONITOR	£135.00	Buy It Now
	Pentium 3 Tower System DVD CDRW 17" & more	**£200.00**	14
	Dell P-III 733 Bargain, 256MB, SFF, Dont Miss	£129.99	Buy It Now
	HP Vectra VLi8 SFF System & 17" Sony T'tron	£104.00	18
	P3 FULL Tower Server DVD CDRW 768Meg 19"	£170.10	15
	MEGA VALUE PC, MONITOR, WINDOWS XP & FREE P&P	£399.00	Buy It Now

Older but still-functional computers are regularly replaced by individuals and industry alike. Shop around at an online auction site like eBay and you'll certainly find some bargains. Look out for pitfalls, though: an office-based machine may lack a sound card and speakers, and you should check whether the hard disk has been wiped clean of software.

PART

Where to shop

Several types of retailer are contenders for your component cash.

Computer superstores

Superstores cater more for people in the market for a ready-made computer or perhaps replacement drive or peripheral than the screwdriver-wielding DIY system-builder. Prices can be exceptionally good on certain lines – take advantage of special offers – but extras like printer cables can attract premium rates.

High street independents

A mixed bunch, in our experience. Many smaller shops are staffed with clued-up enthusiasts happy to offer advice and help you with a purchase. Others are not.

Mail order/web vendors

Having lower overheads than 'real' shops, mail order and internet companies (often one and the same) should be able to offer better prices. They generally do just that, but remember to factor in delivery charges. Some also offer OEM goods, so check whether you're about to order a boxed, consumer-friendly retail product with a manual – or a drive-in-a-bag.

Dabs.com is one of the largest online high-tech retailers in the UK. Its extensive Dabsvalue range includes unbranded OEM-style products at rock-bottom prices.

Superstores like PC World offer a good selection of DIY components alongside complete computer systems. Check the Bargain Zones for the best deals.

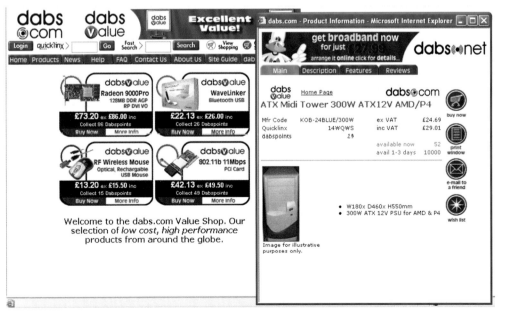

Snapping up bargains at a computer fair stall. See Appendix 4 for details of websites that list local markets.

Computer fair

Computer fairs are held regularly up and down the country. Here you will find the best prices of all, as long as you're prepared to haggle a little. However, the prospect of handing over a large wad of cash to a trader you fear you may never see again is rather daunting. Our advice is to leave your wallet at home the first time you visit your local fair. Get the feel of the place, note the traders' names and jot down some representative prices. You can compare these with shop prices later. By all means have a chat with a few traders and suss out who's prepared to offer free advice and a no-quibble return guarantee.

Official monthly fairs are policed by the organisers, and regular traders do tend to be trustworthy. You will certainly find OEM stock at a fair, and also salvaged components plucked from old PCs. If you need a stick of SD-RAM for an old motherboard, a fair is a good bet – as indeed it is for that old motherboard in the first place.

Golden rules include:

- Only deal with traders who openly display a landline telephone number (not just a mobile number) and address.
- Establish your right of return with the trader before paying, and check how you would go about making a return. Will you have to wait a month or more before you see the trader again?
- Keep all packaging and receipts.

B-grade stock

Damaged goods, items returned by customers without the original packaging, end-of-line components that have to make shelf room for newer stock, used systems sold off by companies upgrading their IT departments ... all manner of functional but not-quite-perfect items qualify as 'B-grade'. The one constant factor is that this stuff is sold at a healthy discount.

You should get a guarantee of sorts with a B-grade item – perhaps 30 or 90 days – and (a matter of importance) any deficiencies should be clearly stated at the point of purchase. You have every right to get your money back if your purchase is dodgy in any way you weren't adequately forewarned about.

Take care, though. A monitor with a cracked screen isn't a terribly bright buy, nor is a fire-damaged power supply unit. But a sound card sold without a box, cables, drivers or manual might be a sensible cost-cutting investment.

And so ...

Above all, shop around. Component prices vary wildly from place to place, often without rhyme or reason. Use a credit card wherever possible to take advantage of the added protection. Bone up on your consumer rights, too, just in case of problems. See Appendix 4 for contacts.

PART

PLANNING THE 'PERFECT' PC

Hard and soft options

In the next section, we'll look at the main components that go together to make a computer. But first you must decide what type of computer you wish to build.

Matching hardware to software

If there was a magic formula – 'to do X and Y buy Z' – we would print it here. Sadly there isn't – but then you can't just walk into a shop and buy the 'perfect PC' straight off the shelf. Nor can we provide you with a definitive buying guide or make specific product recommendations. For one thing, any such advice would be instantly out of date; for another, one of the great secrets of computer design is that it matters far, far less which brand name you buy than whether a given component adheres to industry standards (no proprietary parts here, thank you very much) and has the right specification for its intended purpose. As a system-builder, you have the opportunity – nay, the luxury – of being able to make informed choices about every single part of your computer.

We will talk you through the hardware in Part 2. However, the old adage of horses for courses holds true in the software stakes too: the computer you build must be well-suited to its end use. You don't need a room-sized mainframe to surf the web any more than you need seven satellite speakers and a sub-woofer to keep track of your household finances, but you do need a good deal of processing power and a swanky video card if you want to play computer games (plus a joystick, a powerful sound card and probably a set of headphones to keep the neighbours sweet).

Recommended system requirements

Application type	Typical example	Processor speed (MHz)	Memory (MB)	Hard disk space (MB)	Other requirements
Operating system	Windows Vista Home Basic	1,000 (1GHz)	512	15,000 (15GB)	
Office applications	Microsoft Office 2007 Home and Student Edition	500	256	1,500 (1.5GB)	
Image editor	Jasc Paint Shop Pro	500	128	75	
DVD movie player	CyberLink PowerDVD	400	64	40	DVD drive
Digital video editor	Pinnacle Studio 9	800	512	500	FireWire/USB port to connect a camcorder; lots of hard disk space for storing raw video
Digital media	Roxio Creator 7	500	256	1,000	Recordable CD or DVD drive
Game	Medal of Honor: Pacific Assault	1,500	512	3,000	Video card with 128MB memory
Desktop publishing	CorelDRAW Graphics Suite 12	200	128	250	
Reference	Encyclopaedia Britannica 2004	350	256	400	
Antivirus	Norton Antivirus 2005	300	128	125	
Utility suite	Norton SystemWorks 2005	300	128	150	

In all cases, we assume the presence of a monitor, mouse, keyboard, sound card, speakers, a CD drive from which to install the software and an internet connection.

Changing pace

Computer hardware and software have long played a game of catch-up with one another but not always in the same direction. A few years ago, for instance, it was common for software applications to stretch hardware capability to breaking point. This was especially true in the realm of gaming. Then, for a while, hardware performance leapt ahead and the average desktop PC was much more powerful than we actually needed it to be. Real multitasking, by which we mean being able to run several intensive applications simultaneously, became the norm. Even the humblest mass-production shop-bought system could handle having a web browser, e-mail program, word processor, encyclopaedia and desktop publishing program all open at the same time with surplus capacity aplenty.

By and large, the power balance has shifted little. To make the point, we've listed a few typical applications along with their recommended hardware specifications in the table on p.16. Now, nothing here will remotely stretch any PC that you're liable to buy or build today. Indeed, only one of our sample applications specifies so much as a 1.5GHz processor – they're currently running upwards of twice as fast – and you're unlikely to be pushed for hard disk space with today's 200GB drives. The game's requirement for a hefty video card is the only potential sticking point.

Memory matters

But it's not *quite* as straightforward as all that. Perhaps the most noticeable and certainly the most significant thing about these figures is the importance of memory. The overall quantity of RAM in a system – and to a lesser extent the *type* of RAM chosen – has a huge bearing on that system's overall performance, especially when it comes to multitasking. It's one thing for a computer to run 17 programs at the same time but quite another for it to do so smoothly without locking-up or hanging the system. Given that multitasking is a PC's forte, or should be, and that you shouldn't have to shut down programs A and B before firing up programs C, D and E, it's sensible to install considerably more RAM than you think you need in order to keep things ticking along nicely. Compromise in almost every other area before skimping on memory.

Processors matter too

Moreover, these system requirements mask the fact that in certain key areas software is now once again pushing at the boundaries of hardware. Computer gaming is one obvious area where it's beneficial if not downright essential to have a fast processor, stacks of memory and the very latest souped-up video card at your disposal. Anything less and you won't see your games play to their full potential. Frame rates drop and detail is lost.

But even if you're not interested in games, consider digital video. This is another key area where the possibilities can be hampered by hardware limitations. For instance, a PC makes a fabulous video editing suite if you have a camcorder. You can transfer raw footage to the hard disk and tweak and transform it into a polished home movie. You can then publish your efforts on a website, share them via e-mail or make your own DVDs. Even basic video editing software is spectacularly powerful (including Windows Movie Maker, which comes free with Windows XP and Vista). For the amateur film-maker, these are happy days.

However, the harsh reality is that you need pretty sturdy hardware to work with digital video at a comfortable pace. Just about any PC can edit and produce a movie, but not all can do it while you wait. A slow system will take hours to render a movie (i.e. apply your edits, captions, effects and so forth to raw footage and produce a finished file), and some will need all night and perhaps well into the following morning. While it's engaged in the business of rendering, there's not much else you can do with your computer short of chivvying it along with words of encouragement or, more likely, frustration.

Bottom line: if video is your thing, invest in a speedy processor to cut the waiting time to a minimum.

If movie-making appeals, don't skimp on processing power.

Beige be gone

Much to the amusement of Mac fans, for whom form is almost as important as function, most PC manufacturers now have a stab at making their products attractive. Usually, they fail dismally, but you, the system builder, can have a much better go at this yourself.

We'll build two very different PCs in the course of this book, one of which would look perfectly at home in a living room setting. This is an example of a 'small form factor' PC, which is what you'll likely want if you intend to build a home entertainment centre.

A what, you wonder? Well, odd though it may sound, a suitably configured PC connected to a TV can effectively replace your video recorder, DVD player, stereo system and games console. It can also showcase digital images, import and export media to and from other computers in a home network, and generally function as the very hub of your home entertainment. Forget the keyboard and mouse; all you need is a remote control. Skip to Appendix 2 now for more details. Meanwhile, just bear in mind as you go along that the PC has finally made the leap from the study to the sitting room. You are in the enviable position of being able to design and build an ideal system from scratch.

Our other project PC caters more for future expansion and flexibility but it's no mean looker for all that. It would also be ideally suited to the next step in system-building, which is customising or 'modding' (modifying) a PC for maximum effect. We're talking cut-away Perspex panels that showcase internal neon tube lights, swish water-cooling systems, solid gold heatsinks and that kind of thing. This, though, is subject matter for a different book.

But we're getting ahead of ourselves. Let's turn now to the nuts and bolts that you will use to build your computer.

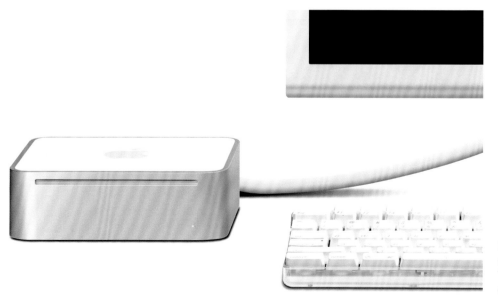

Even now, not many PCs can compete with a Mac for styling. Then again, you can't build your own Mac.

PART 2 **Choosing your hardware**

Motherboard	22
Processor	34
Memory	39
Case	45
Power supply unit	48
Hard disk drive	51
Sound card	56
Video card	59
Optical drives	63
Other possibilities	67
The perfect PC	72

Inevitably this section gets rather technical, but as always we'll focus on what you really need to know and resist wallowing in the mire of jargon and the inner workings of microelectronics. You don't need to know that Intel's 4004 processor ran at a clock speed of 108KHz to appreciate that a top-end Core 2 Duo processor running at 3.67GHz is great for demanding applications but overkill for email.

PART 2 **Motherboard**

The single most important piece of hardware that you will buy is the motherboard – the very heart of your system. The processor plugs into it, drives connect to it with cables, expansion cards live in special slots and everything else, from the mouse to the printer, is ultimately connected to and controlled by the motherboard. If you buy a PC from a shop, chances are you'll never think about or even see the motherboard; but when you build a system from scratch, it must be your primary consideration. Everything else follows from here.

A sample motherboard
Here's a close look at a motherboard like the one we'll be using in the first of our projects.

Memory slots	For installing memory modules
Processor socket	For installing the processor
Chipset (Northbridge)	The motherboard's control centre
Parallel	For connecting a printer
PS/2 (2)	For connecting a mouse and keyboard
S/PDIF in/out	For importing and exporting digital audio signals
RJ45 (2)	For connecting a wired local area network (LAN)
USB (4)	For connecting peripheral devices
Audio (6)	For connecting speakers (7.1 surround sound), a line-in device and a microphone
Wi-Fi	For connecting a wireless networking receiver
PCI Express 16x	For installing a video card

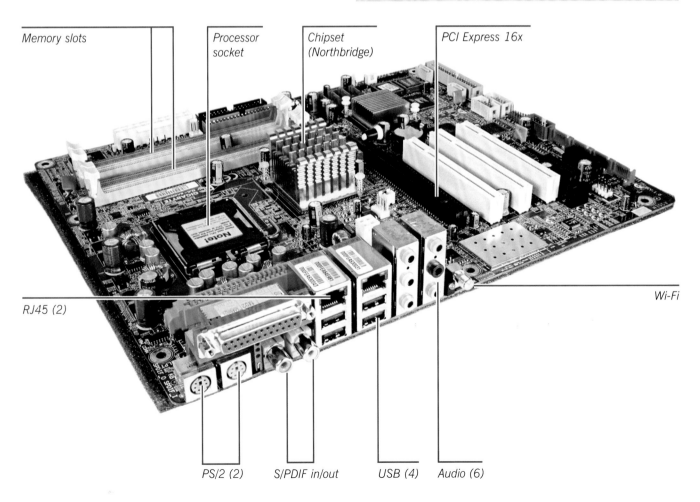

Memory slots · Processor socket · Chipset (Northbridge) · PCI Express 16x

RJ45 (2) · Wi-Fi

PS/2 (2) · S/PDIF in/out · USB (4) · Audio (6)

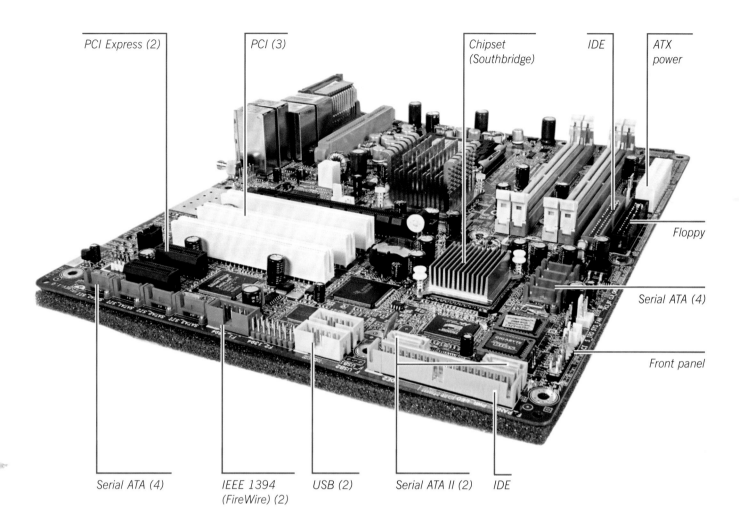

PCI Express (2) PCI (3) Chipset (Southbridge) IDE ATX power

Floppy

Serial ATA (4)

Front panel

Serial ATA (4) IEEE 1394 (FireWire) (2) USB (2) Serial ATA II (2) IDE

QUICK Q&A

I'm considering a motherboard that claims to be 'legacy-free'. It sounds like a bonus but what does it mean?
It means it has no serial, parallel, mouse or keyboard ports and nowhere to connect a floppy disk drive! This might be a good thing but only if you already have or intend to get a USB mouse, keyboard, printer, etc. and don't mind going without a floppy drive. It's certainly the way of the future. For this project, we couldn't quite bring ourselves to ditch these legacy interfaces just yet.

PCI (3)	For installing standard expansion cards
PCI Express (2)	For installing the latest, fastest expansion cards
Serial ATA (8)	For connecting new-style hard drives
IEEE 1394 (FireWire) (2)	For connecting via a FireWire cable to a drive or device
USB (2)	For connecting via a USB cable to a drive or device
Serial ATA II (2)	For connecting high-speed new-style hard drives
IDE (2)	For connecting old-style hard drives
Front panel	For connecting lights and buttons on the front of the case
Chipset (Southbridge)	The motherboard's control centre
Floppy	For connecting a floppy drive
ATX power	For connecting the power supply unit

And another one

This motherboard is an older model but representative of the kind of thing you could easily pick up for a song at a computer fair. We've highlighted the key differences.

AGP	This special slot is used to install the video card. Gradually, the AGP standard is being superseded by the superior PCI Express standard.	Memory slots	The difference here is not obvious to the eye but the newer motherboard can run memory in dual-channel configuration whereas this model can not. For the benefits, see p.42.
PCI	This motherboard has six PCI slots for adding expansion cards, whereas the newer model on the previous pages has but three. However, the newer model also has two PCI Express slots which can host faster, more powerful expansion cards. It also has both wired (LAN) and wireless (Wi-Fi) connections built-in, plus a powerful on-board multi-channel audio chip with a stack of inputs and outputs. This means that you simply don't need as many expansion cards.	IDE	There are two IDE sockets on this motherboard, each of which can host two hard drives or optical CD/DVD drives. The computer can thus have a maximum of four internal drives. On the new model, we still find the IDE sockets, but these are rapidly disappearing in favour of the Serial ATA standard (for which there are no fewer than ten sockets). It's useful to have an IDE socket or two around, if only for reusing existing hard or optical drives, but SATA is the way forward.
Processor socket	Here we see a Socket 478 socket for a Pentium 4 processor. On the newer motherboard, this has been replaced by the LGA775 Pentium 4 socket. As we shall see, the design of processor sockets (and, before that, slots) is ever-changing, which generates a whole bunch of compatibility issues.		

see p.42.

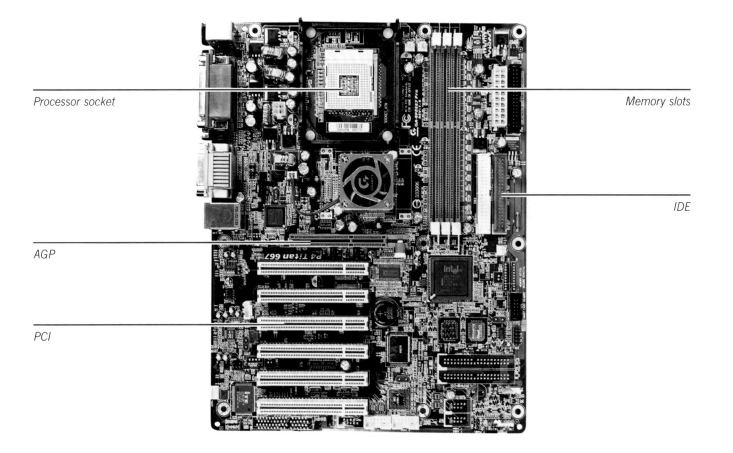

Processor socket

Memory slots

AGP

IDE

PCI

Form factor

This is a fancy way of describing a motherboard's size and shape, important because it involves industry-wide standards and ties in with the computer case and power supply. Form factors have evolved through the years, culminating since 1995 in a popular and flexible standard known as ATX. Not just one ATX standard, of course: there are MiniATX, MicroATX and FlexATX motherboards out there, all progressively slimmed-down versions of full-size ATX. The upside of a smaller motherboard is that you can use a smaller case and reduce the overall dimensions of your computer; the downside is a corresponding reduction in expandability. A full-sized ATX motherboard can have up to seven expansion slots while a MicroATX motherboard is limited to four.

Should you have a tape measure handy and wish to do some checking, here are the maximum ATX motherboard board sizes as specified by Intel:

ATX	305mm	x	244mm
MiniATX	284mm	x	208mm
MicroATX	244mm	x	244mm
FlexATX	229mm	x	191mm

One technical benefit of ATX over the earlier BabyAT form factor from which it directly evolved is that full-length expansion cards can now be fitted in all slots; previously, the location of the processor and memory on the motherboard meant that some slots could only take stumpy (not a technical term) cards. Another is the use of a double-height input/output panel that lets motherboard manufacturers build-in more integrated features. All in all, it's a definite improvement.

But from your point of view, the main attraction has to be the guarantee that any ATX motherboard, including the smaller versions, will fit inside any ATX computer case. That's the beauty of standards.

The most recent mainstream addition to the form factor parade is BTX (Balanced Technology Extended). This has a leaner, flatter form factor compared to ATX, and is specifically designed to facilitate adequate cooling in smaller computers, especially those designed for home entertainment. A BTX motherboard comes in three variations:

BTX	267mm	x	325mm
MicroBTX	267mm	x	263mm
PicoBTX	267mm	x	203mm

Beyond BTX, you can also buy Mini-ITX motherboards from a manufacturer called VIA (**www.viaembedded.com**). These are square in shape, 170mm x 170mm, and designed primarily for squeezing into strictly non-standard computer projects. As Wikipedia (**http://en.wikipedia.org/wiki/Mini-itx**) puts it:

> Enthusiasts soon noticed the advantages of small size, low noise and power consumption, and started to push the boundaries of case modding into something else – building computers into nearly every object imaginable, and sometimes even creating new cases altogether. Hollowed out vintage computers, humidors, toys, electronics, musical instruments, and even a 1960s-era toaster have become homes to relatively quiet, or even silent Mini-ITX systems, capable of many of the tasks of a modern desktop PC.

For examples and inspiration, see **www.mini-itx.com**.

Next in line comes the even smaller 120mm x 120mm Nano-ITX form factor. Like Mini-ITX, this is developed exclusively by VIA with the aim of making even smaller, but still fully functional, PCs possible.

A really very tiny indeed 12cm-square Nano-ITX motherboard from VIA.

The chipset

The real meat of a motherboard resides in its chipset: a collection of microchips that together control all the major functions. Without a chipset, a motherboard would be lifeless; with a duff chipset, it may be inadequate for your needs. Indeed, as one motherboard manufacturer explained it to us, the chipset *is* the motherboard: don't ask what this or that motherboard can do – ask instead what chipset it uses and there you'll find your answer.

So what does a chipset do, precisely? Well, at one level it controls the flow of data between motherboard components through a series of interfaces. Each interface, or channel, is called a bus. The most important buses are:

FSB (Front Side Bus) The interface between the Northbridge component of the chipset and the processor.

Memory bus The interface between the chipset and RAM.

AGP (Accelerated Graphics Port) The interface between the chipset and the AGP port. This is gradually disappearing from motherboards as more and more video cards are designed for the PCI Express slot.

PCI (Peripheral Component Interconnect) bus The interface between the chipset and PCI expansion slots. Pretty much any expansion card can be installed here, including sound cards, network cards and TV tuners. The exception is a video card, as these are, or were, designed for the higher bandwidth AGP interface. Like AGP, PCI is gradually giving way to PCI Express.

PCI Express bus The interface between the chipset and PCI Express expansion slots. There may be two separate buses determined by the bandwidth of the slots. For instance, the motherboard may have a 16-speed PCI Express slot for the video card and one or more slower slots for standard expansion cards.

IDE (Integrated Drive Electronics) bus The interface between the chipset and hard/optical drives.

SATA (Serial Advanced Technology Attachment) bus An alternative interface between the chipset and hard/optical drives which will eventually completely replace the IDE bus.

And then there are buses controlling the floppy disk drive, parallel and serial ports, USB and FireWire, integrated audio, and more.

Here we have a Pentium 4 processor (left), an 82925XE Northbridge or Memory Controller Hub chip (top right) and an ICR6H Southbridge or Input/Output Controller Hub chip. Which is quite some mouthful. But put them together and you'll have a motherboard with an Intel 925XE chipset.

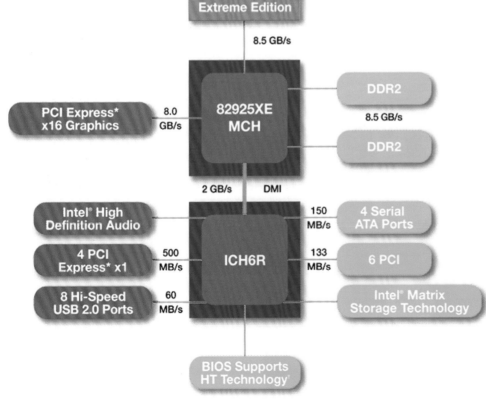

The same chipset viewed schematically. Note how the Northbridge (MCH) and Southbridge (ICH) chips have different responsibilities.

Bus bandwidths

Not all buses are equal. Far from it, in fact: they operate at different speeds and have different 'widths'. For example, the basic single-speed (1x) AGP specification has a clock speed of 66.6MHz (usually expressed as 66MHz). This means that over 66 million units of data can pass between the video card and the chipset through the bus per second. However, the AGP bus transfers 32 bits of data (that's 32 individual 1s and 0s) with every clock cycle, so the true measure of the bus is not its speed alone but rather the overall rate at which data is transferred. This is known as the bandwidth of a bus. In this case, 32 bits pass through the bus 66 million times per second. This equates to a bandwidth of 266MB/sec.

Just to be clear, using round figures, here's the sum:

66,600,000 clock cycles x 32 bits = 2,131,200,000 bits/sec

There are 8 bits in a byte (B), so this equals 266,400,000B/sec

There are 1,000 bytes in a kilobyte (KB), so this equals 266,400KB/sec

There are 1,000 kilobytes in a megabyte (MB), so this equals 266MB/sec

Looked at another way, the AGP bus transfers sufficient data to fill a recordable CD every three seconds.

It's also possible to run the AGP bus up to eight times faster, which boosts the bandwidth to over 2 gigabytes per sec. This is the kind of speed you need for playing games. By contrast, the PCI bus runs at only 133MB/sec. This is fine for many purposes but not for three-dimensional video.

Now consider the bandwidth of an 800MHz front side bus on a motherboard designed for a Pentium 4 processor. The bus itself is 64 bits wide – that is, 64 bits are transferred every second – and the clock 'ticks' 800 million times per second. This equates to a bandwidth of 6,400MB/sec, or very nearly fast enough to fill a DVD with data in a second.

Some buses can transfer data two, four or eight times per clock cycle, which effectively doubles, quadruples, etc. the overall bandwidth. The new PCI Express standard allows for multiple 'lanes' which pump data in a number of simultaneous streams. The upshot is that PCI Express is vastly superior to that of PCI or even AGP 8x-speed.

If all this makes your head spin, put away your calculator and consult the following table instead. We'll save the thrill of memory bus bandwidths for later (see p.43).

Some bus bandwidths

	Bus name	Bandwidth (MB/sec)
FSB (Pentium 4 and Core Duo)	400MHz	3,200
	533MHz	4,266
	800MHz	6,400
	1,066MHz	8,500
Expansion slots	PCI	133
	AGP	266
	AGP 2x	533
	AGP 4x	1,066
	AGP 8x	2,133
	PCI Express 1x	500
	PCI Express 2x	1,000
	PCI Express 4x	2,000
	PCI Express 8x	4,000
	PCI Express 16x	8,000
Drive interfaces	IDE/ATA-33	33
	IDE/ATA-66	66
	IDE/ATA-100	100
	IDE/ATA-133	133
	SATA I	150
	SATA II	300

Chipset architecture

We needn't linger on the physical design of chipsets except to comment briefly on the terminology you are likely to encounter:
- **Northbridge** The primary chip in a chipset, it typically controls the processor, memory and video buses.
- **Southbridge** A second chip that typically incorporates the PCI, IDE/SATA and USB buses.
- **Super I/O** A third, subsidiary chip that usually supports the floppy disk drive, serial ports and a parallel port, and sometimes also the mouse and keyboard ports.

However, these associations between bus and chip are far from immutable. Moreover, Intel recently switched to a 'hub architecture' where the Northbridge chip is called the Memory Controller Hub and the Southbridge is the I/O Controller Hub. AMD, that other processor-producing giant, refers to Northbridge and Southbridge chips as the System Controller and Peripheral Bus Controller respectively. More importantly, the latest Athlon 64 processor family incorporates the memory controller within the processor, thereby releasing the Northbridge chip from much of its responsibility.

From the buyer's perspective, it matters more what a chipset offers overall than how it does it.

Processor and memory support

The two most important questions with any motherboard, and hence computer, are which processor family and what kind of memory does it work with?

For instance, if you decide that you want to build a Pentium 4-based system, you'll need a motherboard with either a Socket 478 or a Socket 775 to house it; and if you want an Athlon-based system, you'll be looking for a Socket 939, 940 or 974. So far, so confusing. It gets all the more so when you factor in the many possible permutations of memory support, including bus speed, number of slots on the motherboard and whether it offers single-channel or dual-channel performance. We'll cover all of this in due course.

Need a further complication? Intel makes its own chipsets, which means it's easy to compare like for like, but AMD largely relies on third-party manufacturers to come up with compatible chipsets for its processors. There's nothing wrong with AMD's stance on this – and indeed it opens the market to chipset manufacturers which would otherwise be squeezed out by Intel's dominance – but it does make motherboard comparisons slightly trickier.

A Socket 939 Athlon 64 processor. We'll use this later in our small form factor PC project.

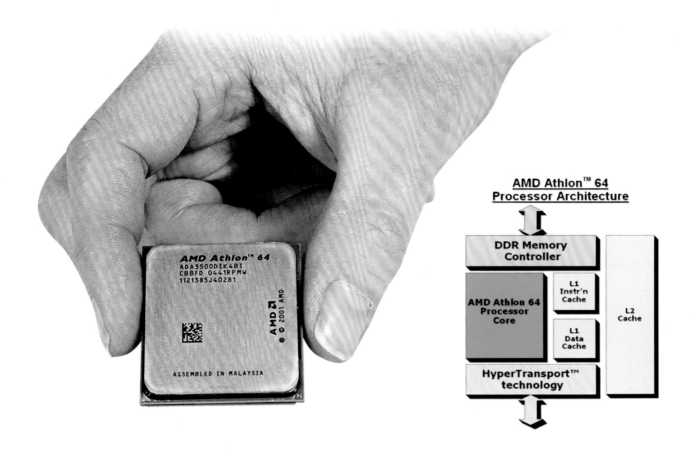

Integrated multimedia

Another important feature of motherboards that again depends upon the chipset is the presence or otherwise of 'onboard' or 'integrated' sound and video. An integrated sound chip means that the motherboard can handle audio playback and recording without the need for a separate sound card. That is, you simply connect speakers and a microphone to outputs and inputs provided by the motherboard. Integrated video means you don't need a separate video card.

The attraction of this approach is primarily one of reduced cost: a motherboard with integrated sound and/or video saves the system-builder having to shell out for one or two pricey expansion cards. A motherboard with integrated multimedia features is thus a smart buy, right?

Well, not necessarily. Remember, we're building the 'perfect PC' here, one requirement of which is that it must be able to adapt to your changing needs. The drawback with integrated multimedia is that it potentially limits your upgrade options. Audio is rather less of an issue than video. Sound cards are always designed for the PCI expansion slot so it's possible to upgrade to a more powerful card later, assuming there is a free slot on the motherboard. The slight complication is that you must

disable the integrated sound chip before your sound card will work (see p.135).

It is also possible to disable integrated video in favour of an expansion card – but where will you install it? Some motherboards with integrated video have a vacant AGP or, more recently, PCI Express, slot for just this purpose, in which case there's no problem: simply disable the chip and install your video expansion card. However, others have no such slot, in which case you are, quite frankly, stuffed. Without a free slot, your only real option would be to install a slower PCI video card, but this would almost certainly be a downgrade. Unless you are very, very confident that you will never wish to upgrade your PC's video capabilities – in particular, that you'll never play computer games or change from an analogue to a digital monitor or wish to run two monitors simultaneously – only consider a motherboard with integrated video if it also has a vacant AGP or PCI Express slot. A small saving now may have serious consequences later.

Of course, there is another advantage to integration, namely reduced size. With the current trend towards smaller, sleeker, lighter, prettier PCs, it makes sense to incorporate as many functions as possible into the motherboard.

When both video and audio output are embedded on the motherboard, as in this small form factor example, the need for expansion slots is reduced. In fact, you may get away with none at all.

Sizing up the specifications

Intel chipsets
What we need here are some concrete examples. We've picked six Intel chipsets and listed their main features in order to highlight the differences between them.

	Intel P965 Express	Intel 925XE Express	Intel 925X Express	Intel 915P	Intel 915GL	Intel 865P
Processor support	Core 2 Duo, Core Duo, Pentium D, Pentium 4	Intel Pentium 4	Intel Pentium 4	Intel Pentium 4	Intel Pentium 4	Intel Pentium 4
Processor socket	775	775	775	775	775	478
Front Side Bus (MHz)	1,066/800	1,066/800	800	800/533	800/533	533/400
Memory (RAM) support	Dual-channel DDR2	Dual-channel DDR2	Dual-channel DDR2	Dual-channel DDR2 or DDR	Dual-channel DDR	Dual-channel DDR
Memory bus (MHz)	800/667/533	533/400	533/400	533/400 (DDR2); 400/333 (DDR)	400/333	333/266
Memory slots	4	4	4	4	4	4
Maximum installable memory (GB)	8	4	4	4	4	4
PCI slots	3	6	6	6	6	6
PCI Express 16x-speed (for video card)	1	1	1	1	-	-
PCI Express	3	4	4	4	4	-
AGP slot	-	-	-	-	-	1
IDE sockets	1	2	2	2	2	-
SATA sockets	6	4	4	4	4	2
Integrated audio	Yes	Yes	Yes	Yes	Yes	Yes
Integrated graphics	-	-	-	-	Yes	-
Integrated LAN	Yes	Yes	Yes	Yes	Yes	Yes

A word of explanation
If you know what you're looking at and what you're looking for, it's possible to get lots of useful information from bare specifications like these. Let's look at the first of our examples, the P965 Express chipset. When we're looking at its specifications, what exactly are we looking at?

Processor support This tells you what make and type of processor the motherboard supports. When you're building a desktop system, this almost always means an Intel Core 2 Duo, Core Duo, Pentium or Celeron processor, or an AMD Athlon or Sempron. Generally speaking, older chipsets don't support the latest processors, so while a recent Intel P965 chipset is designed for the new Core 2 Duo chips and also works with the older Core Duo, Pentium D and Pentium 4 chips, the older 915P chipset only supports the Pentium 4.

Processor socket This tells you what kind of socket the motherboard has. In our table we can see there are two possibilities: Socket 775 and the older Socket 478. Some older Pentium 4 processors use yet another design, Socket 423. The important thing is to know what kind of socket your motherboard has, because this tells you what kind of processor you need to buy.

Front side bus (MHz) This is the speed at which the processor communicates with the chipset and the memory, and the higher the number the more efficient the processor runs. You'll see that the figures range from 400MHz to more than 1,000MHz, and as you've probably spotted already the processors to the left of our table have faster FSB speeds and are, therefore, more powerful than the ones on the right.

Memory (RAM) support You'll find a full explanation of memory on pp.39–44, but for now it's worth noting that there are two main flavours of RAM: DDR and DDR2. There are two ways of using RAM, too: single-channel mode and dual-channel mode. At the time of writing, dual-channel DDR2 RAM delivers the best performance and newer chipsets are designed to take full advantage of that performance.

Memory bus (MHz) As with the front side bus, this is a speed rating – but this time it's for memory. If your budget permits, it's a good idea to get memory that runs at the fastest possible speed your motherboard can handle; for example, in the case of our P965 Express chipset that would mean 800MHz memory. You'll find that motherboards often support more than one memory speed, though, so if you can't afford the very fastest memory you can always get slightly slower RAM just now and upgrade it later if you need to.

Memory slots This tells you how many memory modules you can fit in your motherboard. It's rare for manufacturers to offer fewer memory slots than the chipset can handle.

Maximum installable memory (GB) This tells you how much RAM you can put in your PC and, as you can see, recent chipsets support a massive 8GB of RAM. That's impressive, but actually buying 8GB of RAM will put a big dent in your wallet. For everyday use, 1GB is ideal and even hardcore gamers are unlikely to need more than 2GB. However, it's worth making sure your PC has room for more memory if you need it in the future.

PCI slots This tells you how many PCI slots the motherboard can support and it's one area where different manufacturers offer different amounts – so if you've got existing PCI cards you'd like to use in your new PC, make sure you study the motherboard specification carefully to make sure your chosen board has enough expansion slots.

PCI Express 16x-speed (for video card) The latest and greatest video cards use high-speed PCI Express slots, which deliver the best possible performance. The previous AGP standard is dying out, and it's becoming a rare sight in motherboards.

PCI Express In addition to the slot for a PCI Express graphics card, recent motherboards also include PCI Express slots for other add-ons. It's a good idea to get a motherboard that supports the older PCI standard and the newer PCI Express standard so you can reuse old cards while still being able to upgrade in the future.

AGP slot See PCI Express 16x-speed above.

IDE sockets IDE interfaces are used to connect storage devices such as DVD writers and hard disks but, like AGP, they're dying out – this time, in favour of the better Serial ATA (SATA) standard. Don't despair if your perfect motherboard doesn't have IDE sockets and you want to use an IDE device, though: you can get an adapter that fits an IDE drive to a SATA interface.

SATA sockets As IDE fades into history, SATA is taking its place. It's a very good idea to ensure your chosen motherboard has several SATA sockets.

Integrated audio Most motherboards now include integrated audio, which means you don't need a sound card in order to play music or listen to audio on your PC. That doesn't mean you shouldn't consider a separate sound card, though, as we'll discuss on p.57.

Integrated graphics As you'd expect, integrated graphics mean you don't need a video card – it's all there on the motherboard. But – and it's a very big but – integrated graphics is often rubbish. An integrated graphics system is fine for two-dimensional work such as spreadsheets and email, but if you want to play games or experience Windows Vista's eye candy in all its glory you'll find that even the best integrated graphics systems are hopelessly inadequate.

Integrated LAN Why waste a spare PCI or PCI Express slot on a network card when you can have networking built-in to your motherboard? Most motherboards include support for networking and, in many cases, an Ethernet port that enables you to connect to a local network without installing any additional hardware.

TECHIE CORNER

Chipset drivers You can't upgrade the chipset on an old motherboard but you can and should upgrade the chipset drivers periodically. Sometimes, motherboards are rushed to market and the software that controls the chipset – and hence the entire computer – doesn't work as it should. Sometimes it's downright broken. A driver update is often sufficient to bring the chipset up to speed and hence make the difference between a useful motherboard and a waste of money. Driver updates can also improve chipset performance in a key area such as integrated video. Pay occasional visits to the motherboard or chipset manufacturer's website and look for downloadable driver updates. We should also point out that the risk of running into driver and performance problems is significantly higher if you buy the very latest motherboard and/or chipset on the market, particularly when it's a motherboard manufacturer's first outing with that particular chipset. Why not let others have the headaches and plump for an almost-but-not-quite-spanking-new chipset where early teething troubles will have come to light and (hopefully) been remedied at source?

Intel, AMD and picking the perfect processor

As we've mentioned, Intel's arch-rival AMD does things slightly differently. That means you can't put an AMD chip in a motherboard designed for Intel chips and vice versa but, more importantly, it means that direct comparisons between the two firms' hardware are impossible. You'd have more luck comparing apples and badgers. However, although Intel and AMD use very different chip technology there's not much difference between the things you'll find on their respective motherboards. You'll still get SATA sockets, memory slots, PCI Express slots and so on, and a motherboard based around AMD technology will look like and work like one based on Intel technology.

So which should you choose – AMD or Intel? The short answer is 'whichever you prefer', but the long answer is – surprise! – slightly longer.

AMD doesn't use clock speed to advertise its chips. Instead, it uses a performance rating, a number that shows its performance compared to a Pentium 4 – so an Athlon 64 X2 5000+ has a clock speed of 2.6GHz, but AMD reckons it's the equivalent of a Pentium 4 running at 5GHz.

Unfortunately, there's no such thing as a 5GHz Pentium 4, so the performance rating figure isn't much help. What it can help you do, though, is compare speeds of different processors from the same family – so an AMD chip with a PR rating of 5000+ is likely to be a good deal faster than one with a rating of 4000, provided everything else (such as cache memory) is equal.

Another thing you can do is compare the two firms' products in real-world scenarios. That's exactly what the PC buffs at ExtremeTech did and they found that, in the ultra-demanding game Half-Life 2, the £130 AMD Athlon 5000+ processor delivered similar in-game performance to the £300 Intel Core 2 Duo E6700 processor. However, it's important to note that those results were when the game ran in high detail mode; at low detail, the Intel processor was considerably faster. The Intel chip was also faster at other tasks such as encoding video and rendering complex 3D images.

We think the best idea is to decide what your budget is and then see what AMD and Intel offer in your price bracket. Once you've done that, have a look at a site such as **www.extremetech.com** and see how your shortlisted processors perform in real-world tests.

Chipset Conundrums

If you're considering an Intel-based PC, choosing a motherboard is straightforward enough: just find the right Intel chipset and everything follows from that. You'll find full details of Intel's chipset range at **www.intel.com/products/chipsets**. However, if you'd rather build an AMD-based system you'll need to delve a little deeper and find out what motherboards are available for your chosen processor.

That's something you should do anyway, because motherboards are not created equal. Different firms implement chipsets in different ways, so one firm might offer four PCI slots while another's otherwise identical motherboard offers six, or it might offer four USB ports while a rival firm's board gives you eight. There can be other differences too. Some motherboards supplement their audio connectors with digital outputs that you can connect to high-end audio equipment, while others have built-in wireless networking. Even within their own ranges, manufacturers have a seemingly endless list of motherboards based around a standard chipset but with each one offering slightly different connections or designs.

What that all means is that while it's important to choose the right chipset, unfortunately you'll still need to wade through different motherboards' specification sheets to make sure you're getting the one you really want. If you understand what the different specifications mean and have a clear idea of the kind of PC you want to build, picking the right motherboard is easy – and once you've chosen that, everything else falls swiftly into place.

For every Intel processor, there's an AMD alternative. This is the AMD Athlon 64 X2, a direct rival to dual-core Intel chips.

PART  # Processor

The processor or central processing unit (CPU for short) is your PC's brain, and its speed is a key factor in the overall performance of your PC. It's also a crucial marketing tool for PC manufacturers, who pack their ads with claims such as 'The fastest processor the world has ever seen!' or 'The processor's so fast, it'll do things before you've even decided to do them!' Of course, the ads have a point: when it comes to your new computer, you should get the fastest processor you can find. Shouldn't you?

Not necessarily. There are two very good reasons why you should ignore the very latest CPUs. The first is that they're far too expensive and the second is that you almost certainly don't need and won't benefit from them.

Let's say you want to play Half-Life 2 on your new PC and you want superbly smooth performance – so you look at the Intel Core 2 Extreme X6800, which is a mighty quad-core processor with a clock speed of 2.93GHz apiece. That's bound to be a beauty, isn't it? Not so fast, because there are two pretty major problems with that chip. The first and most obvious problem is that it costs £620 and the second problem is that it's useless for Half-Life 2.

Intel's Core Duo is the replacement for the Pentium processor and it has already evolved into the Core 2 Duo processor and the Core 2 Extreme processor.

If you buy an Intel processor in retail packaging, the box also includes the processor heatsink and cooling fan. If you go for a cheaper OEM version, the heatsink isn't included.

At the time of writing Half-Life 2 doesn't support multi-core processors, so your fancy Core 2 Extreme's massive power won't be used. By comparison, you can get a Pentium 4 chip running at 3.2GHz for just £46. That's a saving of £574 and it offers perfectly decent performance in Half-Life 2 as well as everyday computing tasks. If you spend another £200 on a high-end graphics card and some extra RAM, you'll have a machine that, for now at least, blows a Core 2 Duo system out of the water – and you'll still be more than £300 better off than if you'd gone for the cutting-edge chip.

It's an extreme example, we know, and by the time you read, this Half-Life 2 will no doubt take full advantage of dual-core and quad-core technology. However, it shows that buying the fastest processor around doesn't always mean you'll get the best performance for the things you'll actually be doing.

Processor evolution

The history of processors is long and duller than dishwater, so let's stick to the things you actually need to know. The table below shows recent Intel processors from the Pentium 4 onwards, together with the key features of those chips. Where the table shows more than one figure the lowest figure is for the earliest, slowest chips and the highest is for the latest, fastest ones.

Processor	Type	Clock speed[1] (GHz)	L2 Cache[2] (MB)	FSB (MHz)	Socket
Core 2 Duo	Dual core	1.8–2.67	2–4	800–1,066	Socket 775
Pentium D	Dual core	2.8–3.6	2–4	533–800	Socket 775
Pentium 4	Single core	1.3–3.8	.025–2	400–1,066	Socket 423/478/775

[1] Clock speed is a measure of a processor's work rate, expressed in millions (MHz) or billions (GHz) of cycles per second. The higher the clock speed, the more instructions the processor can carry out per second, although that's not the whole story: the FSB speed and other components, such as memory, also affect the processor's real-world performance. Remember too that clock speeds for dual-core systems are per core. Another issue to consider is that different processor architectures means that comparisons between different processor families aren't possible. For example, Core 2 Duo clock speeds are clearly lower than those of later Pentium 4s, but they don't have the Pentium 4's famously inefficient Netburst architecture. That means they need fewer instructions to do identical tasks and, as a result, they're much more efficient and run much more quickly.

[2] Level 2 cache is a sliver of extremely fast memory that lives inside the processor and speeds up communication between the CPU and the chipset, so the more you have the merrier you will be. On some multi-core processors, the cache figures are per core.

As you can see, processors have evolved in three key areas: clock speed, cache size and FSB speeds. However, something else has happened too, which is that each processor line eventually reaches the limits of its underlying technology. The Pentium 4 hit the buffers at 3.8GHz, by which point its descendant, the dual-core Pentium D, had already appeared. The Pentium D took its place for a while, but today the more efficient and more powerful Core 2 Duo is at the top of the tree (there was also a Core Duo but it was very short-lived). Eventually that too will be phased out, with the four-core Core 2 Quad Extreme taking its place.

A similar evolution has taken place in AMD processors, with Athlons becoming Athlon XPs, Athlon 64s and today's dual-core Athlon 64 X2s. As with Intel chips, over time AMD has boosted its processors' cache memory and evolved its motherboard socket designs, so the most recent AMD chips use the AM2 socket design while older chips need Socket A motherboards.

Whether you go for an Intel or an AMD chip it's worth bearing in mind that the faster processors in their ranges use more power and emit more heat than the slower ones, so they may require more powerful power supplies and better cooling systems than their cheaper, less powerful siblings.

In addition to the two firms' desktop processors, Intel and AMD both make mobile versions of their processors. These are primarily designed for laptops where battery life was more important than outright performance. Intel had the Pentium M and today, the Core 2 Duo Mobile; AMD has the Sempron, the Mobile Athlon and the Turion range. Unless you're building an ultra-small PC where energy efficiency is your number one priority, you'll be better off with a dedicated desktop CPU. We'll look at mobile processors in more detail in a moment.

Two cores or not two cores?

Comparing processors used to be easy: a 2GHz chip was twice as fast as a 1GHz one. However, the current generation of processors boasts dual-core technology, which means that the chip manufacturer has crammed two CPUs onto a single chip. As if that wasn't enough there are quad-core CPUs and eight-core versions won't be far behind. Intel reckons that we may be using 80-core CPUs by 2011. So what does this mean for the budding PC builder?

On paper, a dual-core system should be much faster than a single-core one, so for example a dual-core processor running at 1.67GHz should easily outperform a single-core processor that runs at 2.8GHz. And that's true, provided your software supports it. Both Windows XP and Windows Vista support dual-core technology, but older versions of Windows don't and some games haven't caught up yet.

The main advantage of a dual-core processor is that it can do two things at once. Single-core chips only pretend to multitask, which is why your system often becomes sluggish if you're running two programs simultaneously. You'll notice a big difference between a single-core CPU and a dual-core one when you try to do something demanding while still using your PC, so for example if you're ripping CDs to Windows Media Player while writing an angry letter to the bank, running a full virus scan and downloading files from the internet, a dual-core system will be considerably smoother and more responsive. If you're only doing one demanding thing, such as rendering video, the CPU will use both of its brains at once.

For demanding tasks – editing really big digital photos, working with video, using your PC as a digital video recorder while simultaneously doing the accounts and digitising your record collection – we'd definitely recommend a dual-core processor. However, if money's tight and you don't really need to multitask it might be a better idea to get a really fast Pentium 4 and a motherboard that enables you to pop in a dual-core chip later on.

One of the best things that's happened since the last edition of this book is that processor prices have plummeted, so even recent dual-core chips are affordable: while the fastest Core 2 Duo chips are still over £600, dual-core Intel and AMD chips start at around £100. If you don't want or don't need dual-core processing, Pentium 4s are currently selling for around £40.

Celerons and Semprons

In addition to their main desktop processors, Intel and AMD also make low-powered chips that are particularly well-suited to laptops, budget computers and small form factor PCs. Such processors have different names to their desktop equivalents, so for example the cut-down Pentium chip is known as the Celeron and the cut-down Athlon is the Sempron.

There are two main differences between Celerons or Semprons and their mainstream equivalents. The first is price; for example, at the time of writing, **www.maplin.co.uk** is offering a fairly speedy Sempron 3400 and a motherboard for under £70. That's around the same price as a stand-alone Pentium 4 processor and roughly half the price of a Pentium 4 and motherboard. However, the second and most important difference is performance. Celerons and Semprons have been designed from the outset as low-cost processors and, in order to build chips to a budget, corners have to be cut somewhere.

To use a car analogy, let's say your PC is a Ford Focus. The Celeron and Sempron are the entry-level engines that appear in the cheapest Focuses; while they'll get you from A to B, they're not as swift, as smooth or as efficient as the more expensive engines available. Returning to the world of PCs, that's why the very cheapest PCs you'll see on sale are running Celerons while the ones targeted at power users have the latest Core 2 Duos or Athlon XP chips.

So where have corners been cut? Typically you'll find that such processors have smaller on-board cache memory and slower bus speeds than their big brothers; as a result, they don't offer the same blistering performance. It's not a huge issue for everyday computing, but if you plan to use your PC for demanding tasks such as video editing or cutting-edge gaming then you might find that the low-cost chips don't deliver the performance you need.

Another issue to consider is the processor's support for other bits of your PC. For example, AMD's site shows that its latest Semprons support the PC 3200 standard for memory, which runs at 667MHz. That's perfectly respectable and fine for the majority of applications, but it's not as fast as the newer PC 6400 standard with its 800MHz bus speed. If you want your homebrew PC to use the very latest and fastest memory technology, cut-down processors aren't the way to go.

If you're considering a Celeron or Sempron, the same issues apply as when you're shopping for a Core Duo or Athlon chip: different chips use different sockets and run at different bus speeds, so it's important to choose your motherboard and processor combination carefully to make sure they're a perfect match.

AMD's Sempron and Intel's Celeron processors are cut-down versions of the firms' more powerful processors. They're designed for system builders on a tight budget.

They come in many shapes and sizes but, stylish or otherwise, a heatsink is an essential accoutrement for a hot CPU.

Cooling

Processors get very, very hot when in use and need to be adequately cooled. This usually involves a heatsink unit with a built-in fan that attaches directly to the processor by means of clips. The heatsink has aluminium fins that dissipate heat generated by the hot core of the processor and the fan cools it with a constant flow of air. Many motherboards also have a secondary heatsink to cool the Northbridge chip.

Without a heatsink, a processor would soon overheat and either shut itself down, if you are lucky, or burn out completely and probably take the motherboard with it.

All retail processors ship with suitable units in the box. Indeed, this is one very good reason to pay a little more for the retail packaging. If you source an OEM processor – i.e. one originally supplied to a computer manufacturer and later resold – you will also have to buy a compatible heatsink/fan. This is no great problem but do be sure to get one rated for the clock speed of your processor. It must also be designed for the appropriate socket i.e. a Socket 775 heatsink won't fit in a Socket 478 motherboard.

We cover the installation of heatsinks in detail later. See also Appendix 1 on quiet PCs.

Memory

System memory – Random Access Memory (RAM) – is just as critical a component in your new computer as the processor. More so, even. Too little memory and the fastest processor in the world will choke on its workload; stacks of memory and you can run several software applications at the same time without the system stuttering, hanging or crashing.

At the simplest level, computer applications run in RAM, by which we mean the files required to open and maintain a given program are transferred from the hard disk, where the program is installed, to RAM for the duration of the session. If you turn off your computer or it crashes, RAM's memory is 'flushed' or wiped out, so you have to start again. That's why it's so very important to save your work as you go along. Only then are your changes copied from RAM back to the hard drive for permanent storage.

Let's say you want to perform a sum in a spreadsheet. The spreadsheet program isolates the data required to perform the sum. RAM then sends this data to the processor through the Front Side Bus (or in the case of an Athlon 64 processor, directly via the integrated memory controller). The processor crunches the numbers, comes up with an answer, and sends it back to RAM. Finally, RAM feeds the result to your spreadsheet program and the solution appears on your monitor screen.

It all happens very quickly indeed. However, in all but the most intensive applications, such as real-time video editing, the overall speed of the system is governed far more by RAM than by the processor. When a computer runs painfully slowly, chances are that RAM is the bottleneck, not the processor.

Some memory modules sport their very own heatsinks to help diffuse the heat. Cynics argue that these bolt-on accessories are mainly for show, like go-faster stripes.

Modules

RAM comes in the form of chips soldered to long, thin modules that plug into slots on the motherboard. These modules are remarkably easy to install but buying the right modules in the first place is a more complicated matter.

As mentioned above, any motherboard/chipset supports one type of RAM and one alone. This is not to say that you should buy your motherboard first and then look for compatible memory modules as an afterthought. Quite the reverse, in fact: as soon as you've decided between an Intel or an AMD processor, turn your thoughts to RAM and let this decision govern your choice of chipset (and hence motherboard).

Now, we could fill the rest of this manual with techie talk about memory evolution, error-checking, voltages, transistor counts, latency and so forth, but it would make your eyes glaze over and get us almost nowhere. Let's focus instead on the absolute essentials.

DDR-RAM

When the Pentium 4 first appeared, it was 'optimised' for a special kind of proprietary memory licensed (although not actually manufactured) by a company called Rambus. Marketed as Rambus Dynamic RAM, or RD-RAM, the memory modules use a form factor known as RIMM and require corresponding RIMM slots on the motherboard. RIMMs come in 184-pin, 232-pin and 326-pin variations. However, RD-RAM is now almost completely out of favour so we'll say no more about it.

Athlon XP-based systems have always been built around an altogether different type of memory called Double Data Rate Synchronous Dynamic RAM, or DDR SD-RAM (we'll shorten this further to DDR). This comes in modules called DIMMs, which have 184 pins. Again, the motherboard must have compatible DIMM slots. DDR-RAM is manufactured by many different companies and is relatively cheap. The standard has also evolved to keep pace with faster processors and motherboard buses, which basically means that DDR keeps getting faster. It is still the default memory for an Athlon 64 system. A glance at the chipset table on p.30 will tell you that many Intel motherboards also support DDR modules.

There are 184 pins in this DDR DIMM. DDR memory is compatible with both Intel and AMD processors.

A glance at the chipset table on p.30

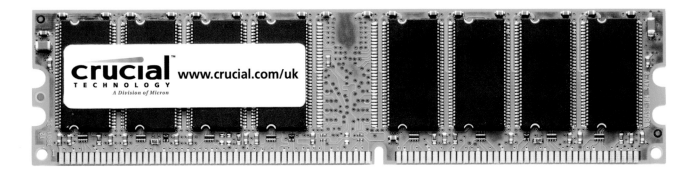

Doubling up

But that's not the end of the story. The speed of a memory module is rated in a similar way to that for processors. That is, the manner in which it transfers data is determined by a clock. This is really a change in voltage in the memory slot from zero to 2.5V at a given rate, or frequency. A clock speed of, say, 200MHz means the frequency changes 200 million times per second. With each change in frequency, or clock cycle, the memory module can send and receive data. Moreover, DDR memory can send and receive data twice per clock cycle (once on the way up, as the frequency rises from 0 to 2.5V, and once on the way back down again). That's why it's called Double Data Rate.

Beyond DDR we find Dual Double Data Rate RAM (DDR2). This comes in 240-pin modules. The main advantage is that DDR2 operates at higher clock speeds than DDR and transfers data four times per clock cycle rather than DDR's twice. This translates to a higher bandwidth in the sense that more data can pass between RAM and the processor every second. However, DDR2 modules suffer notoriously from high latency. Latency is the delay between an instruction being issued and the instruction taking place. For reasons too dull to explore, the first generations of DDR2 modules had such high internal latencies that they were frequently out-performed in practice by DDR. Only recently have low-latency DDR2 modules begun to turn the theoretical advantage of DDR2 into enhanced performance in the real world. DDR2 support is widespread in Intel chipsets and motherboards, but for most Athlons DDR is the default choice. That's starting to change, though, and AMD began offering chipsets with DDR2 support in 2006.

DDR2 boosts bandwidth. It comes in 240-pin modules and can only be installed in a motherboard that explicitly supports DDR2 memory.

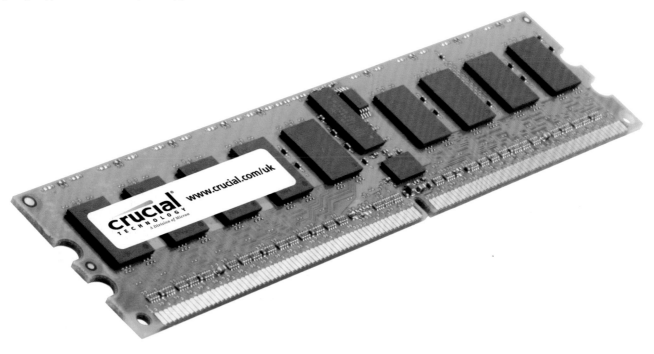

SD-RAM Before DDR2, DDR and RD-RAM, we had humble Synchronous Dynamic RAM. SD-RAM is dynamic because its contents are flushed continually and lost altogether when you turn off your computer; and it's synchronous because it is synchronised for performance with the motherboard's memory bus. DDR and DDR2 are merely enhancements of this original standard.

Presumably there are still motherboards around that support SD-RAM but only on the second-hand market. Suitable memory modules are also very difficult to obtain. Memory is a commodity market where demand drives supply and there's simply no call for fresh SD-RAM these days. However, it looks likely that DDR will gradually be superseded by DDR2 so, even if you are on an extremely tight budget, we'd strongly advise you to forget about defunct SD-RAM and hang on for a DDR bargain. As with every development in computer generations, the previous, still-powerful generation gets marked down in price very, very quickly. This means that high-bandwidth, high-capacity DDR memory modules will soon be cheap as chips.

You can still get hold of SD-RAM for older motherboards but it's not exactly flying out of Taiwan's fabrication plants these days.

Dual-channel memory

In a nutshell, then, you need DDR memory for an Athlon PC and either DDR or DDR2 for an Intel machine, although the very latest Athlon chipsets have moved to DDR2 too.

Ah, but there's yet another factor at play here. Many motherboards support dual-channel memory configurations. The idea is that you can run two modules in parallel at the same time to effectively double the bandwidth between RAM and the processor. The trick is having two memory controllers on the motherboard.

The standard analogy for dual-channel memory is a jammed motorway. Let's say you have three lanes of traffic cruising at 70mph. If you want to get more cars from A to B in a given time, what can you do? Well, first you can increase the traffic flow by raising the speed limit. This is akin to running memory at ever-faster clock speeds. So now you have a three-lane motorway with traffic hurtling along at 140mph. The next option is squeezing more cars into the available space. This is DDR2's approach. Traffic moves at the same speed – 70mph – but now there's twice as much of it. However, the motorway is now running at full speed with no spare room (or safe distance) between the vehicles. What else can you do to shift more traffic?

You can build an identical motorway alongside the first. This is what a dual-channel memory configuration does. Apply the methodology to a motherboard and in theory it shifts twice as much data to the processor and thus does everything twice as quickly. In practice, the benefits are more modest but it's still an increased performance that you can *feel* rather than merely chart in a benchmark test.

The critical thing about dual-channelling is that you must use two identical modules and install them in the correct slots. If you try to dual-channel with modules of different speeds or capacity it will not work.

The Socket 939 design for Athlon 64 processors supports dual-channelling, as does Socket 775 for the Pentium 4.

Bus bandwidths revisited

Of course, there's little point in sending six lanes of high-speed traffic towards a two-lane roundabout. The bottleneck would be horrendous. In a perfect world of perfect motherboards, the bandwidth of the memory bus and the processor bus (FSB) would match perfectly.

Cast your mind back to p.27 and remember that the bandwidth of a bus is determined by an equation:

Clock speed (MHz) x data quantity (bits) x multipliers

DDR and DDR2 RAM have a 64-bit bus width so each unit of data comprises 64 bits (or, if you prefer, 8 bytes). The multiplier relates first to how many times per clock cycle data is transferred. With DDR memory, the multiplier is two; with DDR2, it is four.

So, for instance, what's the bandwidth of a DDR memory module with an internal clock speed of 100MHz?

$$100,000,000 \times 64 \times 2 = 1,600MB/sec$$

(Divide the answer by 8, to convert bits to bytes, and then by 1,000,000, to convert bytes to megabytes).

If you installed two such modules in a dual-channel configuration, you would double the bandwidth to 3,200MB/sec. This perfectly matches the bandwidth of a Pentium 4 processor with a 400MHz FSB (as shown in the table on p.27). That is, the processor and RAM can share data at 3,200MB/sec with no bottlenecks.

You would see this kind of memory module described in a shop as PC1600 or DDR-200, or usually as both:

PC1600 DDR-200

The PC figure tells you the overall bandwidth in terms of MB/sec; the DDR figure reflects the *effective* speed of the memory bus, which is simply the clock speed times the multiplier. In this example, the memory module's true clock speed is 100MHz but this bus runs at 200MHz thanks to double data rate performance.

The DDR figure is the more important one because this tells you at a glance which type of memory is compatible with your motherboard. For instance, when you see a chipset or motherboard that supports 400MHz memory, you know you need DDR-400 modules.

Still, it's all terribly confusing. In fact, it gets worse when you consider DDR2 memory. Because DDR2 transfers data four times per clock cycle rather than twice, you would expect that a DDR2 module with the same clock speed as a DDR module would have twice the bandwidth. In fact, DDR2 runs with slower clock speeds so it all balances out.

For example, the bandwidth of a DDR2 module with a 100MHz internal clock speed is:

$$100,000,000 \times 64 \times 4 = 3,200MB/sec$$

This module would be advertised as:

PC3200 DDR2-400

The real advantage of DDR2 is that the higher multiplier makes it possible to boost the bandwidth without dramatically increasing the clock speed. DDR2 modules also run at a lower voltage than DDR – 1.8V compared to 2.5V – and consequently generate less heat.

Here's a summary of the current possibilities:

Memory name	Internal clock speed (MHz)	Data transfers per cycle	External memory bus speed (MHz)	Bus width (bits)	Bandwidth (MB/sec)
PC1600 DDR-200	100	2	200	64	1,600
PC2100 DDR-266	133	2	266	64	2,100
PC2700 DDR-333	167	2	333	64	2,700
PC 3200 DDR-400	200	2	400	64	3,200
PC3700 DDR-466	233	2	466	64	3,700
PC4000 DDR-500	250	2	500	64	4,000
PC4300 DDR-533	266	2	533	64	4,300
PC2-3200 DDR2-400	100	4	200	64	3,200
PC2-4200 DDR2-533	133	4	266	64	4,200
PC2-5300 DDR2-667	166	4	333	64	5,300
PC2-6400 DDR2-800	200	4	400	64	6,400

Selecting memory

The first rule when buying memory is to get the fastest sort that the motherboard supports. That is, if your motherboard chipset supports both 400 and 533MHz buses, spend that little extra on DDR or DDR2 533 modules. If it also supports dual-channel, buy matching pairs and install them in the appropriate slots (see p.86–7). In fact, we highly recommend that you consider only dual-channel motherboards if you want peak performance. Remember, dual-channel uses standard DDR or DDR2 modules so you effectively get twice the performance for no extra outlay. If you take the DDR2 route, consider buying more expensive low-latency modules for an extra boost.

Here's another recommendation: don't attempt to match memory modules to motherboards yourself. It's a truly fraught process so make it easy on yourself with an online memory configuration tool. With these, you enter motherboard details at one end and at the other end out pops a list of compatible modules.

Let's jump the gun and test one out.

Crucial Technology's Memory Adviser (www.crucial.com/uk) invites you to tell it who made your computer, which isn't a very promising start for a DIY system builder. What it really needs to know, of course, are the motherboard details. If you have a motherboard in mind or if you have already bought one, select the manufacturer here. In this example, it is Gigabyte. In the next couple of steps, select your precise model. Choose carefully.

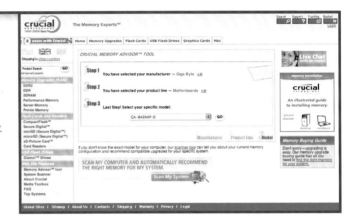

The screen also gives you frequently asked questions, such as whether your motherboard supports dual-channel memory. In this case the answer is 'Yes'. The Memory Adviser helpfully presents a summary of your chosen motherboard's memory support. It's well worth double-checking this against the official specification. Here, for instance, we learn that the motherboard supports up to 4GB (or 4,096MB, which is the same thing) of DDR2 memory in either the PC3200 or PC4300 flavours (a.k.a. DDR2-400 and DDR2-533) in a 240-pin DIMM format.
(What Crucial refers to as PC2 4200 appears in our table on p.43 as PC4300. The terms are interchangeable. The additional '2' in PC2 is also optional.)

At the top of the screen you'll see three memory deals, but if you scroll down there are lots of other memory modules. Choose carefully: this motherboard only supports up to PC4300 memory, so buying the first item – PC8000 – is a waste of money, because it will run at PC4300 speeds. The same applies to option 2 at the top of the screen – it's faster than the motherboard can actually handle. It pays to check these things very carefully when you're on a budget.

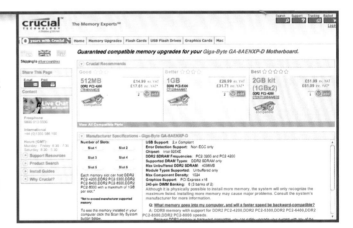

PART  Case

Just as all motherboards adhere to certain industry-standard dimensions, so too do computer cases. Far and away the most common form factor is, again, ATX. You can be sure that any ATX motherboard will fit in any ATX case. That's the kind of simplicity that we appreciate. But that's not to say that all cases are the same.

Towers vs desktops

Far from it, in fact. For starters, you can choose between a tower case or a desktop case. One is tall and narrow, the other squat and wide. We heartily recommend going for a tower case. They are overwhelmingly more prevalent than desktop cases and, in our experience, considerably easier to work with. The exception would be if you're building a home-entertainment-style PC for living room use. In this case, style matters almost as much as function.

You can get full-sized, mid-sized and mini tower cases, which are progressively shorter versions of the same thing. The sole advantage of a low-rise tower is neatness; the considerable disadvantage is a corresponding lack of expansion possibilities. A mini-tower will typically have two or three 5.25-inch drive bays, a mid-tower between three and five, and a full-tower anywhere up to seven. Given that you will probably install a CD-RW drive and a DVD-ROM drive, a three-bay case still has room for one

Here we see a full tower case with a side panel removed and its front fascia on and off.

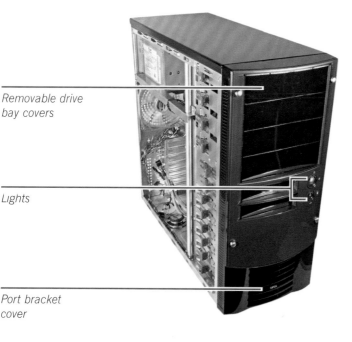

Removable drive bay covers

Lights

Port bracket cover

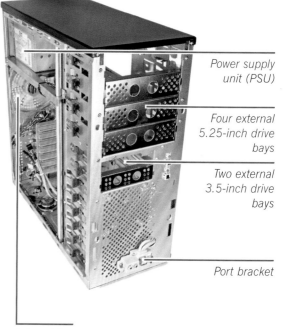

Power supply unit (PSU)

Four external 5.25-inch drive bays

Two external 3.5-inch drive bays

Port bracket

Internal fan

Aluminium cases like this one from Lian-Li are light, strong and cool.

additional device (a sound card breakout box, perhaps) whereas a two-bay case would effectively be full.

Pay attention to 3.5-inch drive bays, too. You'll need at least one for the hard disk drive and another for the floppy drive/card reader. However, we're going to recommend that you install two hard drives and possibly as many as four. Spare internal drive bays thus rank somewhere between desirable and essential.

In short, you want to allow your PC room to grow. Of course, it's always possible to strip the entire innards from a computer and reinstall everything in a larger case should the need arise, but this is about the most drastic and fiddly upgrade you could ever perform. Better, we suggest, to allow for future expansion at the outset.

A non-ATX small form factor platform like this offers little in the way of expansion possibilities, but you may consider that a fair compromise if you need a looker for the living room.

Case features

Drive bays are protected by drive bay covers on the front of the case. These snap-out or unscrew to afford full access to the bay, whereupon you can install an internally-mounted drive.

A case also has a series of blanking plates to the rear that correspond to the motherboard's expansion slots. You'll remove one every time you install an expansion card. Above this is a rectangular input-output (I/O) panel. This is where the mouse, keyboard, parallel, serial and other ports poke through when the motherboard is installed.

On the front of the case, you will find two buttons: the main power on/off switch and a smaller, usually recessed reset button that restarts your computer if Windows hangs. There will be a couple of lights, too: one to show when the power is on and one that flickers whenever the hard disk drive is particularly active. The case may also have an extra opening to accommodate an expansion bracket loaded with audio or USB ports.

Your case may have a single all-encompassing cover that lifts straight off or separate removable side panels. It may be held together with screws, thumbscrews or some arrangement of clips. Internally, you may find a removable motherboard tray. This is a boon, as it's much easier to install the motherboard on an external tray than it is to fiddle around inside the case.

Inside the case, along with the drive bays and a cluster of cables, you'll find a pre-installed fan or two and possibly a mounting area for an optional extra fan. The case will also have a speaker which the BIOS will use to generate beeps (see p.158).

Beyond all of this, designs vary from the standard, boring 'big beige box' look to undeniably funky. Pressed-steel cases are generally cheaper but brushed-aluminium looks (and stays) cooler. Some cases are heavy, reinforced and thoroughly sturdy; others are lightweight, flimsy and easily dented. We would simply advise you to focus on functionality before frills. A full-sized tower case is generally easier to work with, easier to keep tidy internally, more adaptable to customisation and provides better airflow to the motherboard's components.

The same case we saw a moment ago, stripped of its covers and seen from the rear.

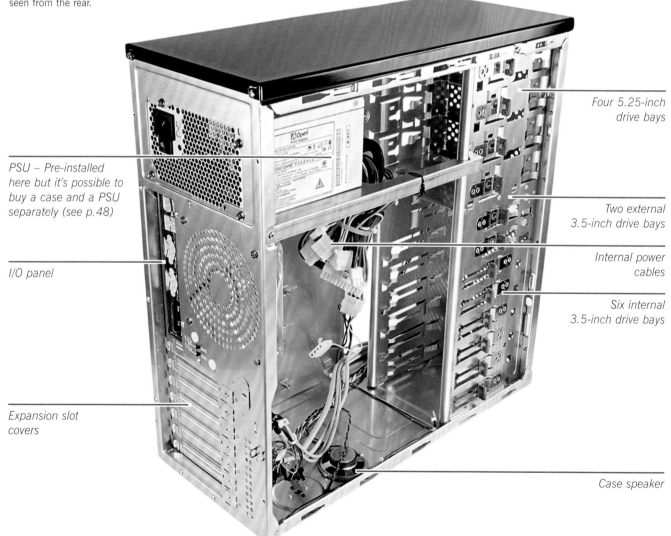

PSU – Pre-installed here but it's possible to buy a case and a PSU separately (see p.48)

I/O panel

Expansion slot covers

Four 5.25-inch drive bays

Two external 3.5-inch drive bays

Internal power cables

Six internal 3.5-inch drive bays

Case speaker

PART 2 **Power supply unit**

The power supply unit (PSU) supplies power to the computer's motherboard and drives. That much is obvious. Less so is the importance of getting the right PSU, particularly when many cases come with an anonymous unit pre-installed. Ignore the specifications here and you risk all sorts of problems. If possible, purchase your case and PSU separately, or at least devote as much care to the PSU as to every other component.

A reliable power supply unit is a must. This ATX model has an adjustable fan speed for quiet running and pumps out 350W.

Compatibility

To go with your ATX case and ATX motherboard, you need an ATX PSU. Virtually all new PSUs comply with the ATX standard, which means it will fit in an ATX case and power an ATX motherboard.

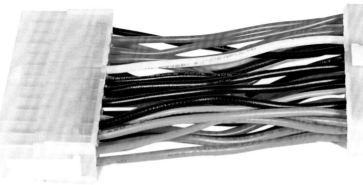

An adapter for converting a 24-pin PSU connector to a 20-pin motherboard.

However, if you are using an Intel processor and a Socket 775 motherboard, take care. You'll need one of the newer PSUs that has a 24-pin power connector rather than the older 20-pin standard. If you intend to reuse an older PSU or if you buy a 20-pin unit and later find that you can't connect it to your motherboard, all is not lost: you can buy an adapter to convert a 20-pin connector to a 24-pin connector. However, this is not advisable unless the PSU pumps out at least 450W of power. We strongly recommend that you buy a new 24-pin PSU instead. Conversely, though, you can also get an adapter to convert a new 24-pin PSU for use with an older 20-pin motherboard, and that's risk-free.

Also ensure that you get a PSU with SATA connectors if you have a SATA-enabled motherboard and SATA hard drives. Again, an adapter or two can save the day but it is better to buy the appropriate equipment in the first place.

We don't recommend buying a second-hand PSU. An under-powered PSU might not supply power-hungry components with the juice they need, particularly if you cram your case full of drives and accessories, and an older unit with a history of hard work behind it is obviously more liable to burn out and die.

An IDE-to-SATA adapter for powering new-style drives from an older PSU.

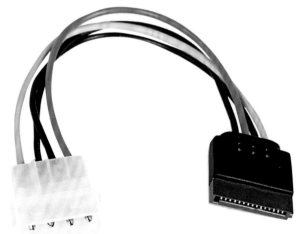

Yet another adapter. This one converts a Molex cable into a pair of SATA connectors.

Power rating

A 250W or 300W PSU is inadequate, 350W is fine and 400W is better still. Simple as that.

Cooling

A PSU has an integrated fan that controls airflow through the computer case. Some also have a second fan that blows cool air at the motherboard. We strongly recommend that you buy a PSU specifically rated for the kind of processor you intend to use.

Noise

A secondary consideration, certainly, but important nonetheless. Some PSUs make a terrible racket while others operate with barely a whisper. If a peaceful PC is important to you, shop around for a quiet device with adjustable-speed fans. See also Appendix 1.

Connectors

The PSU connects directly to each internal drive in your PC and to the motherboard itself, supplying the lot with power. Here's a run through of what to expect.

TECHIE CORNER

AMD used to be very particular about cooling and airflow requirements on PSUs designed for use with its Athlon XP processors. In particular, it recommended the use of a PSU with an air intake on the bottom of the unit, i.e. in the vicinity of the processor. You can find a list of accredited PSUs at **http://snipurl.com/dlpy**. However, with the move to Athlon 64 and 64 FX, the company is now happy for system builders (like you) to use standard ATX PSUs. That said, dual-fan PSUs are still recommended.

	Desirable Version	Undesirable Version	
Rear:			They look about the same! (Differences are brand specific)
Front			Intake only in front is not optimal
Bottom			Bottom intake cools the CPU best

If you're using an Athlon XP processor, don't assume that just any old PSU will do; AMD lays down specific requirements and you'd best buy a unit that abides by them.

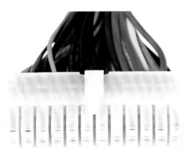

ATX power The main power connector that plugs directly into the motherboard. As mentioned above, the design has switched recently from 20-pin plugs to 24-pin.

ATX Auxiliary A secondary 6-pin power connection required by some older motherboards. If your motherboard has an ATX Auxiliary socket, you must connect this cable.

ATX 12V Some Pentium 4 motherboards require yet another cable connection from the PSU to provide extra power to the processor. However, the latest Socket 775 motherboards dispense with this.

Molex drive connector Used to power hard disk and optical drives.

SATA drive connector Used to power Serial ATA hard drives (and some of the latest optical drives).

Berg drive connector Used primarily to power the floppy drive.

PART **2** # Hard disk drive

You'll want to install a decent-sized hard disk drive (HDD) in your computer, which means anything upwards of 160GB. Digital video, image and sound files certainly eat heavily into disk space – a single hour of raw footage transferred from a digital camcorder requires a massive 13GB – and you'll find more ways than you thought possible of filling a disk with data. True, you can always add a second or third internal or external HDD later if you run out of room, and non-essential material can also be easily archived on recordable CD or DVD media to free up disk space as and when required, but it's only sensible to start with a sizeable disk from the outset.

The good news is that hard disks are relatively cheap, weighing in at under 50p per gigabyte. However, there are other concerns beyond mere storage.

A hard disk drive stores data on high-speed spinning magnetic platters. Remarkably, they last for tens of thousands of hours.

Interface

The two abbreviations you'll come across most frequently are IDE (Integrated Drive Electronics, sometimes prefixed with an extra E for Enhanced) and ATA (Advanced Technology Attachment). Although technically distinct, these terms are used interchangeably to describe the connection between the HDD and the motherboard.

Another common occurrence is DMA (Direct Memory Access, sometimes prefixed with an extra U for Ultra). This tells you that the device can 'talk' to RAM directly without sending data through the processor first, which is a good thing. And then there's ATAPI, which is ATA with a Packet Interface bolted on. This enables optical CD and DVD drives to use the same interface as the HDD.

For many years, motherboards have come with a pair of IDE/ATA connectors labelled IDE1 and IDE2, each of which can support either one or two devices. IDE1 provides the primary channel, to which you would typically connect the hard disk drive, and IDE2 provides the secondary channel, to which you would typically connect the CD and DVD drives.

However, IDE/ATA is on the way out and in its place we have SATA. The S stands for serial. The slowest SATA bus is wider than the fastest IDE/ATA bus, which means that more data can pass between the drive and the rest of the system per second. See the table below. This, though, is a theoretical enhancement that makes little or no difference to actual performance, for reasons which we'll discuss in a moment. The real difference for system-builders is a new cable design. SATA uses a thin, flexible cable instead of the traditional flat ribbon-style cable, which is both neater and better for airflow around the case.

Interface	Also known as	Maximum bandwidth (MB/sec)
ATA-66	ATA-5, IDE-66 or UDMA-66	66
ATA-100	ATA-6, IDE-100 or UDMA-100	100
ATA-133	ATA-7, IDE-133 or UDMA-133	133
SATA-150	SATA I	150
SATA-300	SATA II	300

Data transfer rates

The real-world performance of a drive doesn't just depend on the bandwidth. In fact, many an ATA-100 drive can outpace an ATA-133 device at reading or saving large files. It comes down to a specification called the internal, or sustained, transfer rate. This is a measure of how quickly a drive can read data from its own disks. The bandwidth figures quoted above relate to the external transfer rate but this merely tells you how quickly the drive can shift data out to the main system. Manufacturers are notoriously reticent about sustained transfer rates, one reason being that the figure is significantly lower than the headline-grabbing external interface.

Sustained transfer rates peak between around 40–70MB/sec, which is some way short of even the ATA-100 standard's external transfer rate, let alone SATA's 150MB/sec and up. The drive may be perfectly capable of pumping out huge volumes of data but this is of questionable value if it can't gather this data at anything like the same rate. The bottleneck is the drive itself, not the interface.

Cables

For an ATA-66 or faster HDD, use only an 80-conductor IDE/ATA cable. This has the same plugs as the older 40-conductor style and looks very similar, but it incorporates twice as many wires within the ribbon. The extra wires are essentially non-functional, but they reduce interference and help preserve a true signal.

Two drives sharing an IDE/ATA channel on the motherboard must be allocated master and slave status in order that the motherboard can tell them apart. This is achieved with little plastic jumpers on the drives. If you mistakenly set both drives to Master or to Slave, neither will work. However, with an 80-conductor cable you can set all drives to the Cable Select position and forget about them: the cable sorts out master/slave status automatically.

With SATA, it's simpler still. This is a one-drive-per-channel technology, which means no more sharing, no more master/slave status, and no more jumpers.

A 40-conductor IDE/ATA cable, an 80-conductor IDE/ATA cable, and a SATA cable.

TECHIE CORNER

As an alternative to IDE/ATA or Serial ATA, you might consider SCSI (Small Computer Systems Interface). This is a high-speed interface suited to all manner of drives and devices, from scanners and external CD drives to internal hard disk drives. The main advantage is one of performance: a SCSI drive is usually faster than an IDE/ATA drive, with data transfer rates across the bus of up to 160 or 320MB/sec (Ultra160 and Ultra320 respectively). Again, however, the interface speed is largely theoretical; the drive's real-world performance depends more upon its sustained transfer rate, and this will not necessarily be faster than an IDE/ATA drive. Moreover, gigabyte for gigabyte, SCSI drives are very much more expensive than IDE/ATA devices. We can't, in all honesty, claim that the extra expense pays significant dividends.

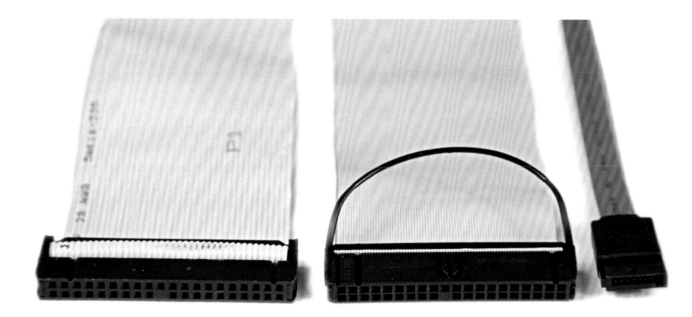

Other considerations

Cache A slice of memory built into the drive that holds frequently accessed data in a buffer state. This saves the drive having to continually re-read from its disks. A 2MB cache is a good minimum; 8MB is desirable.

Spindle speed The rate at which the drive's disks spin. This has a bearing on how quickly the device can read and write data. 5,400rpm is adequate for a low-specification system but we'd recommend a 7,200rpm drive. As a not-entirely-consistent rule, a 7,200rpm drive will have a faster sustained transfer rate than a 5,400rpm drive.

S.M.A.R.T. An error-checking procedure that tries to predict when a hard disk drive is about to fail or, at least, has an increased risk of doing so. This gives you time to make a critical data backup. You need two things: a S.M.A.R.T.-enabled drive and either a motherboard BIOS with native support for S.M.A.R.T. or a standalone software program that works in tandem with the drive.

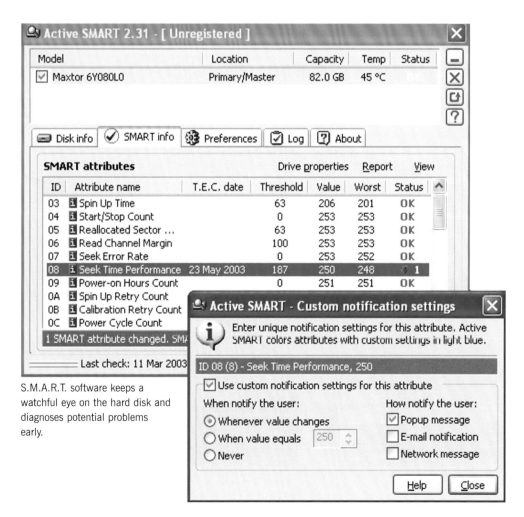

S.M.A.R.T. software keeps a watchful eye on the hard disk and diagnoses potential problems early.

RAID

Once the preserve of network servers, a RAID (Redundant Array of Independent Disks) setup is now a possibility for many home/office computers. Essentially, a RAID-supporting motherboard lets you use two or more hard disk drives simultaneously to 'stripe' or 'mirror' data.

With striping, also called RAID Level 0, the computer treats each hard disk as part of a whole. Two 60GB drives, for example, effectively become a single 120GB drive. Data is then distributed evenly between the drives, resulting in faster read/write performance. The risk is that a single drive failure means all data is lost.

With mirroring, or RAID Level 1, every file you save to the primary hard disk is simultaneously copied to every other drive in the system. Such duplication offers a high level of data security and reliability but, because the additional drives simply mirror the contents of the primary drive, you don't get the benefits of additional storage capacity. It's an expensive way to safeguard your files.

If you reckon RAID is for you, look for a chipset/motherboard with RAID drive controllers and RAID-compatible BIOS. Some motherboards support striping and mirroring simultaneously (Level 0+1), although for this you would need a grand total of four drives.

A RAID adapter expansion card provides additional sockets for connecting hard disks. This is a SATA model. However, an ever-increasing number of motherboards have built-in support for RAID and provide all the sockets you need.

PART  **Sound card**

Before buying a sound card, ask yourself four questions:

Do you want to play music on your computer?

Do you want to play games on your computer?

Do you want to watch movies on your computer?

Do you want to record music on your computer?

The answers determine what kind of sound card you need.

A sound card such as Creative Labs Audigy 4 has more bells and whistles built into it than many an entire computer of yesteryear, and even comes with an external input/output box and a remote control. Essential equipment for the musician or gamer but only true audiophiles get really worked up about the nuances of one sound technology over another.

Music

For music playback, be it audio CD tracks, MP3 files or any other format, stereo is usually sufficient. Most music even today is still recorded in stereo so adding a few extra speakers here and there doesn't actually enhance it. That said, some audio hardware and/or software can 'upmix' a stereo signal to give an illusion of surround sound.

Games

Here you'll benefit from a multi-channel surround sound (or 'positional audio') system. This is where the audio signal is composed of several discrete channels relayed to satellite speakers strategically positioned around the listener.

The sound card should also support one or more of the popular sound technologies, including DirectSound3D, THX, A3D and EAX. The trouble is – as you will know if you've ever given this field more than a cursory glance – that there are so many competing, evolving and incompatible standards out there that it's simply impossible to get a sound card that supports everything and to keep up! Still, just about every game will play in a fall-back DirectX mode and should even install the requisite software for you.

Movies

DVD movie soundtracks are almost always encoded in 5.1 or 7.1 surround sound with Dolby Digital or DTS technology. This means you need five or seven satellite speakers plus a subwoofer (for low-frequency tones) to hear the full effect. You also need a sound card that can either decode the signal itself or pass it through to a separate decoder unit that sits between the card and the speakers.

Recording

Should you wish to connect a MIDI keyboard or other controller to your computer, you'll need a MIDI input. This is pretty much standard; most sound cards provide a combined MIDI/games controller port. Look for ASIO support, too. This is a driver standard that reduces the delay, or latency, between, for example, pressing a key on a MIDI keyboard and the sound registering with the recording software. Latency used to make multi-track recording a real pain but ASIO drivers help enormously.

Integrated vs expansion card

But here's the big question: do you need a sound card at all? Many motherboards provide perfectly acceptable, even stunning, multi-channel audio output by means of an embedded audio chip

Fancy a cinema in your sitting room? Then you'll need a multi-channel sound system with speakers to do it justice.

QUICK Q&A

I picked up this old sound card from a stall but it doesn't fit in my PC!
That will be because you were sold an obsolete ISA card and your motherboard has only PCI expansion slots, as is the norm these days. See if you can exchange it for a PCI card.

(which can be a standalone component or part of the main chipset). For instance, look for AC'97 or Realtek ALC880 support.

The traditional disadvantage with integrated audio is that you only get a limited number of inputs and outputs – typically a few on the motherboard's I/O panel and perhaps an optional port bracket – and you may have to fiddle with software settings in order to connect the full array of speakers. However, we have seen more and more motherboard manufacturers wising up to these shortcomings and providing a full array of audio connectors on the I/O panel. Dropping outmoded interfaces like the parallel and serial ports helps to free up space.

Integrated multi-channel audio has advanced to the point where it rivals expansion cards in almost every area. Only the musician or someone with very particular connectivity requirements really need look further.

In any event, we suggest that you select a motherboard with integrated audio and see how it suits. If you decide that you need a separate sound card after all, it's an easy upgrade to perform. Expansion cards always use the PCI interface these days. PCI Express versions will be along shortly but don't be fooled into thinking you need one: sound cards require very little bandwidth so there's no reason whatsoever to splash out on PCI Express when PCI is more than adequate.

When space is tight, sound ports typically double up duties. Two of the three ports here (lower right corner) function either as speaker outputs or as line and mic inputs, depending upon how the audio driver software is currently configured.

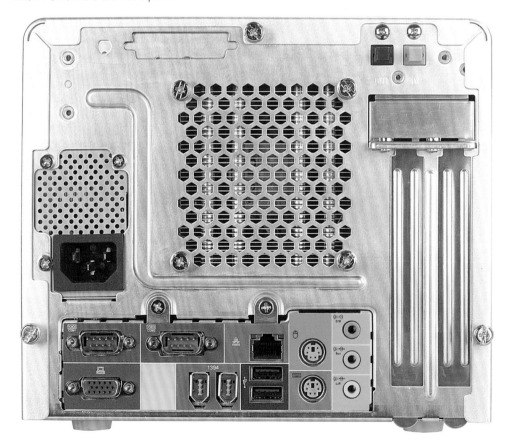

PART 2 **Video card**

Like sound technology, the computer graphics arena is a fast-moving, ever-shifting, highly-competitive minefield of acronyms, abbreviations and indecipherable, incompatible 'standards'. Still, on we go ...

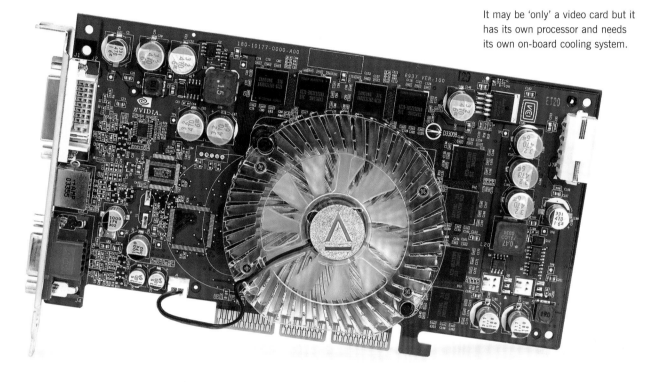

It may be 'only' a video card but it has its own processor and needs its own on-board cooling system.

Chipsets

Just as a motherboard is built around a chipset, so a video card (or graphics card, as they are also called) has at its heart a graphics processing unit (GPU). This is supported by a hefty slice of dedicated RAM located on the card itself. In effect, the video card is like a mini-computer in its own right, albeit with the very specific task of generating images on a monitor screen.

The two main GPU players right now are NVIDIA and ATI. Keep an eye on the latest Matrox cards, too, especially if you need multiple monitor support (see Quick Q&A on p.62).

2D/3D

All you need for a two-dimensional display at a comfortable resolution of 1,024 x 768 pixels is a mere 4MB of on-card memory. That's fine for office applications, image editing, web browsing and pretty much everything else. However, computer games demand a lot of additional power. 32MB is about the minimum but you'll find most cards now have 128, 256 or even 512MB of RAM.

3D isn't really three-dimensional, of course, but the card uses complex lighting and texture techniques to create a realistic illusion of depth.

Interface

As we saw earlier, AGP (Accelerated Graphics Port) is a special slot on the motherboard reserved for video cards. At 266MB/sec, the single-speed version has double the bandwidth of PCI; at 8x-speed, it tops 2GB/sec. However, the AGP interface is now rapidly being replaced by PCI Express running at 16x-speed. This provides a massive 8GB/sec of bandwidth, which promises to prove a real (not just a theoretical) advantage for playing fast 3D computer games.

But PCI Express cards don't yet come cheap. Some motherboards have both AGP and PCI Express 16x-speed slots, in which case you can take your pick.

We said earlier that we are reluctant to recommend integrated video unless the motherboard also has a free expansion slot and we reiterate that now. It simply doesn't make sense to rule out future upgrades from the outset. However, if you are sure that 3D isn't your thing, or the children's, or the grandchildren's, a motherboard with an integrated video chip is certainly an economical purchase.

Sitting proudly in its PCI Express slot, this video card boasts up to 8GB of bandwidth – and a truly bizarre cooling system.

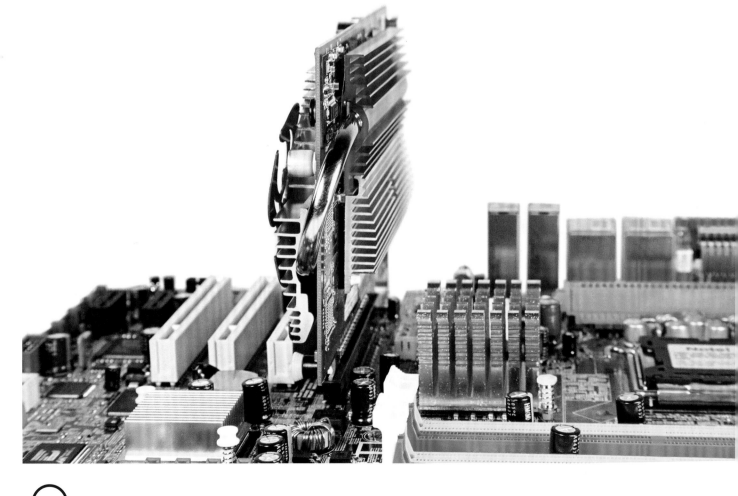

DVI

A video card is a natively digital device that has to perform a digital-to-analogue conversion in order to send a signal that an analogue monitor can understand and display. This conversion degrades the integrity of the signal to a degree (a small degree, admittedly). Worse, modern flat-panel TFT monitors are actually digital devices at heart so the analogue signal has to be re-converted back to digital upon receipt. This is patently crazy, hence the evolution of a purely digital connection between video card and monitor: DVI (Digital Visual Interface).

When you connect a DVI monitor to a DVI video card, the digital signal is transferred from one to the other more or less wholesale. The result is a truer image with more faithful colour representations. Better still, there's no need to mess around with fiddly monitor controls in pursuit of a perfect picture: the card and monitor work in harmony to display the best possible image automatically.

The traditional 15-pin VGA plug and socket are disappearing in favour of DVI so a DVI-capable video card is a sensible purchase. If you have an analogue monitor with a VGA cable, a simple adapter will get it connected until such time as you upgrade to a digital display.

QUICK Q&A

I've just been reading up on computer game standards and now my head hurts. What should I do?

Buy a PlayStation2? Sorry to sound flippant but computer gaming gives us a headache too. With a games console, you know that any game designed for that particular platform – PlayStation, Xbox, GameCube or whatever – will work straight out of the box with no configuration. Which is not to say that we are anti-computer gaming; it's just that we prefer the simplicity of a dedicated gaming platform, just as we'd rather watch a DVD movie on a television screen than a monitor.

If your video card has only one port, make sure that it's DVI. This one has also has VGA, which is handy, but the alternative is a DVI-to-VGA adapter.

This video card ships with a plug-in adapter that provides ports for connecting external video devices.

Optional extras

As well as broadcasting pictures to a monitor, a video card can be put to other uses. These include:

- **TV-out** Hook up your computer to a TV set instead of a monitor to watch movies on the big screen.
- **Video in** Transfer video from an analogue video device such as a VCR or a camcorder onto the hard disk.
- **TV tuner** Connect an aerial and you can watch TV on your PC.
- **Dual-monitor support** Connect two monitors simultaneously for a widescreen effect.

For full details of what's possible with a video card and for tests and reviews of all the latest hardware, go to **www.tomshardware.co.uk/graphics**

? QUICK Q&A

My video card has both VGA and DVI ports. Can I connect two monitors?
Probably not. Many video cards provide two outputs but these are mere alternatives i.e. you can use one port or the other but not both simultaneously. If you want to run two monitors, the usual approach is to install a PCI video card alongside the AGP card and connect one monitor to each. Windows recognises this arrangement automatically so configuration is straightforward.

However, you can also get 'dual-head' and 'triple-head' video cards that incorporate all the circuitry required to run two or three monitors through the same bus. This is actually preferable because you get an AGP-generated display on each monitor and it doesn't eat into your allocation of PCI slots.

For the best results with multiple-monitor displays, invest in a specialist card like the Matrox Parhelia. One DVI channel can be split to run two monitors, meaning that up to three can be powered simultaneously from a single AGP interface.

SLI technology – what it is and why you should immediately forget about it

'Imagine tearing through today's most advanced PC games with an unheard of 48 gigapixels per second of raw graphics performance, 6 teraflops of compute [sic] power, 96 pixel pipes and an astounding 2GB of on-board graphics memory,' babbles graphics card manufacturer NVIDIA at **www.slizone.com/object/slizone_gf7950_gx2.html**. 'You don't have to imagine any more – this kind of power is available TODAY!' No, we've no idea what NVIDIA's on about either, but we do know it's got something to do with SLI.

Scalable Link Interface (SLI) is a way to run two extremely powerful NVIDIA graphics cards in the same PC (rival firm ATI has its own version of the technology, which it calls CrossFire). The benefits to the manufacturer are obvious – instead of selling you one stupidly expensive graphics card, SLI means it can sell you two – but what are the benefits to you? Er, none really. Unless your software's designed for SLI (or CrossFire), you can actually end up with poorer performance than with a single graphics card and, unless you're a keen PC gamer with a monitor the size of a house or you've been given the job of animating Shrek 4 from scratch, you almost certainly don't need SLI.

SLI (and rival standard CrossFire) enables you to connect two graphics cards together. It's almost certainly overkill for home computing.

PART 2 Optical drives

The 'average' shop-bought PC these days has two optical drives: a CD-RW drive and a DVD-RW drive. In fact, the rapid uptake in recordable DVD after a shambolic start has been the only significant shift in optical technology recently, to the point where a DVD writer is *de rigueur* and no doubt about it.

Interface

If your motherboard has two IDE/ATA controllers, as is the norm, you can connect two devices to each. Typically you would install the HDD on the motherboard's primary channel (IDE1) and have your CD and DVD drives share the secondary channel (IDE2).

You don't need to use 80-conductor cables with optical drives (see p.53) but it does no harm and gives you the useful option of being able to set the jumpers on both devices to Cable Select.

However, as we have discussed already, the IDE/ATA interface is gradually being phased out in favour of SATA. Although CD and DVD drives have no practical use for the increased bandwidth that SATA provides, it is possible – and indeed sensible – to buy a drive with a SATA socket rather than IDE/ATA. This ensures that you'll be able to reuse the drive in a future PC that uses a SATA-only motherboard. It also saves all that fuss with jumpers and helps keep the inside of your computer case tidy and cool.

To play music on audio CDs or a DVD movie soundtrack through the computer's speakers, you can connect the drive's analogue or digital audio output to one or other of the sound card's audio inputs (or directly to an analogue or digital socket on the motherboard if your motherboard has integrated audio). That said, in virtually every case you can forego this cable completely and allow the computer to extract audio directly and digitally through the IDE/ATA or SATA bus (see p.137).

Looking at a typical drive from a less flattering angle, from left to right we see the digital (small) and analogue (larger) audio cable sockets, the jumper pins, the IDE/ATA ribbon cable socket and finally the 4-pin Molex power socket.

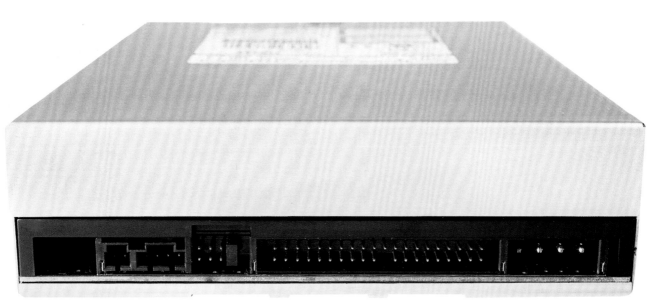

CD and DVD

A plain CD-ROM drive can read and play CDs but a CD-RW drive lets you make your own. There are two types of media: CD-R discs that, once full, can not be erased or re-recorded and CD-RW discs that can be reused time and time again.

To read DVD discs, be they data, audio or movie, you need a DVD-ROM drive. But if you want to make your own DVDs, you need a DVD writer – and that's where the fun begins ...

Recordable DVD

There are three distinct DVD recording technologies around: DVD-R/-RW (the 'dash' or 'minus' formats), DVD+R/+RW (the 'plus' formats) and DVD-RAM. The R stands for recordable, in the sense that you can use a blank disc just once; while RW denotes Rewriteable, which means you can erase a disc and reuse it.

Each format has its pros, its cons, its proponents and its detractors.

- To backup and safeguard your own files, any format will do just fine. You needn't worry about compatibility issues if sharing your discs is not an issue.
- To turn a video file into a DVD movie that you can watch on the DVD player in your living room, check which recordable DVD technology the player can read and buy a drive to match. DVD-R/-RW has the widest drive/player compatibility, DVD+R/+RW runs a close second and DVD-RAM is incompatible with most DVD players. That said, in recognition of recordable DVD's popularity, more and more DVD players are offering support for all formats. This means that compatibility is no longer the burning issue it once was.
- Many DVD drives now also support all recording formats, which means you can throw just about any recordable media at them and emerge with a perfectly playable DVD. A multi-format drive is a smart choice.

Recording/writing/burning (one and the same) your own audio, data and video CDs is a breeze. Windows XP supports basic CD recording without the need for any third-party software.

- So too is a drive that supports dual-layer recording in the +R format. When paired with a dual-layer disc, this increases capacity from 4.7GB to 8.5GB. That equates to more movies or files per disc and, importantly, makes for easier backups. And with a double-sided dual-layer disc, you can go all the way to 17GB per disc.
- All DVD writers can record CDs, too. You may therefore feel that a single drive is all you need in new system. Indeed, if you're building a small form factor PC, one drive is all you'll have room for. The only real disadvantage is that you can't perform direct disc-to-disc copying when you have but the one drive. However, this limitation is not fatal: any decent recording software will extract an 'image' (copy) of the original disc, save it on the hard drive, then copy it onto a blank disc later.

A recordable DVD drive looks just like a CD drive but there's a power of technology packed into that case. This is a dual-layer multi-format model.

Speed

Here's something not to worry about: read and write speeds. All recordable drives carry a cluster of speed ratings which refer to how quickly they burn discs of different formats. The very first generation of CD-ROM drives read data at a top rate of 150KB/sec and faster speeds are expressed as a multiple of this speed: 2x, 4x and so on. For instance, a 40x-speed drive can read data at 6,000KB/sec. Drives are usually slowest at writing data (or recording – it means the same thing) but there's not much in it these days.

DVD-ROM drives are also speed-rated. However, the base speed here is 1,385KB/sec, which is about nine times faster than an original CD drive. A 16x-speed DVD drive thus reads data at a rate of over 21MB/sec. Not that you really need this kind of speed in everyday use; a 1x DVD drive is adequate for movie playback. Again, recording speeds are slower but usually plenty fast enough.

By way of example, here are the speed ratings for the drive we use in our two PC projects later:

Media	Read speed	Write speed
CR-ROM	48x	-
CD-R	48x	48x
CD-RW	48x	24x
DVD-ROM	16x	-
DVD-R	16x	16x
DVD-RW	16x	6x
DVD+R	16x	16x
DVD+RW	16x	8x
DVD+R dual-layer	16x	4x

QUICK Q&A

What are the benefits of a high-speed drive?

Well, you can install software programs and burn your own CDs and DVDs more quickly in a fast drive. That's about it. The fact is that optical drive speeds have reached a practical plateau and are unlikely to get any faster until the next optical technology comes along.

Meanwhile, the faster a recordable drive runs, the greater the risk that the computer will fail to provide it with sufficient data to keep its laser burning continuously. The slightest pause or stutter used to mean a wasted disc and you'd have to start again. However, just about every drive now comes with some form of buffer under-run protection that alleviates the problem. You can minimise the risk further by leaving your PC to concentrate on the task at hand when it's busy burning a disc rather than attempting to multitask.

Buffer under-run protection (or burn-proofing) is built into most CD and DVD writers these days and dramatically reduces the number of spoilt discs they churn out.

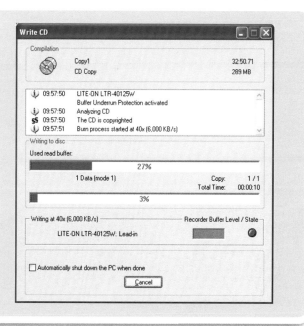

DVD is dead. Or is it?

At the time of writing, two new kinds of disc hope to replace DVD in everything from PCs to video players: Blu-Ray and HD-DVD. Both formats mean new hardware – neither format will play in a CD or DVD drive, and you'll need a Blu-Ray drive for Blu-Ray discs and an HD-DVD drive for HD-DVD discs. While they offer a number of advantages over standard DVDs, we'd recommend steering clear of both formats for a little while longer. We'll explain why in just a moment, but first – what are they?

Blu-Ray and HD-DVD are based on DVD technology, but while DVD drives use a red laser to read data the newer formats use blue lasers. Blue lasers have a shorter wavelength than red ones, and that means data can be crammed much more tightly into a blue-laser disc than a red-laser one. In practice, that means HD-DVDs can store between 15GB and 30GB on a single-sided disc, while Blu-Ray manages between 25GB and 50GB.

That extra capacity makes Blu-Ray and HD-DVD ideal for storing high-definition movies, which can't fit on a standard DVD – and that's where the problems lie, because the film studios can't agree on which format is best. Some film studios quite rightly point out that Blu-Ray offers more storage and faster data transfer speeds, so they'll be releasing their movies on Blu-Ray discs; other studios equally rightly point out that HD-DVD is much cheaper to make, so that's the format they'll use for their movies. The same's happened in the world of technology, with Blu-Ray creator Sony and its friends at Apple plumping for Blu-Ray but Microsoft and its allies embracing HD-DVD instead.

In other words, we've got a format war – just like with the VHS and Betamax video formats back in the '80s. It's possible that neither new format will succeed – DVD-Audio discs and Super Audio CD discs were supposed to replace the humble music CD, but didn't. More likely, one format will thrive and the other one fail. Unfortunately, nobody really knows which one will be the winner, so when it comes to upgrading we'd suggest sitting this battle out until a victor emerges.

Blu-Ray and its rival HD-DVD format offer much more storage than standard DVD discs, but for now they're both battling for supremacy.

PART  # Other possibilities

There's no shortage of potential add-ons and optional extras for a fledgling computer. Here we discuss a few essentials and suggest some other possibilities.

Modem

Before broadband internet access became widely available, a modem was a must-have – you couldn't get online without it. However, these days broadband is cheaper and much, much faster than old-fashioned dial-up internet access; as a result, the only time you need a traditional modem is if you live in a remote bit of the country where broadband isn't available.

If you get broadband, you might still get a modem – a cable modem for cable broadband or an ADSL modem for telephone line broadband – but they're not really modems as we know them; they're usually devices that plug into a spare USB port and which connect to your broadband socket in the wall. In most cases you get them free when you sign up with a broadband Internet Service Provider.

A DSL or cable modem will generally be supplied as part of any broadband internet deal but you may need to install your own analogue modem for dial-up internet access.

Network Interface Card (NIC)

It often makes sense to link computers together in a local area network (LAN). This lets you easily exchange files, share an internet connection and remotely access devices like printers and drives. At its simplest, you can connect two PCs by installing a NIC in each and connecting them with a 'crossover' Category 5 Ethernet cable. To network three or more computers, you need standard non-crossover Category 5 cables with a network hub or switch between them to act as traffic-master. Windows has all the software you need so network configuration is virtually automatic.

When shopping for a NIC, your main choice is between a card that supports Ethernet (or 10BASE-T), Fast Ethernet (100BASE-T), or Gigabit Ethernet (1,000BASE-T). These have theoretical maximum bandwidths of 10Mb/sec, 100Mb/sec and 1,000Mb/sec respectively. Dual- or triple-speed Ethernet PCI cards are commonplace, cheap and ideal.

However, many, probably most, motherboards now provide native support for networking – you'll find an RJ-45 socket or two on the rear input/output panel – and this makes a standalone NIC redundant. Check before you buy.

A network interface card is not required when networking capability is provided by the motherboard.

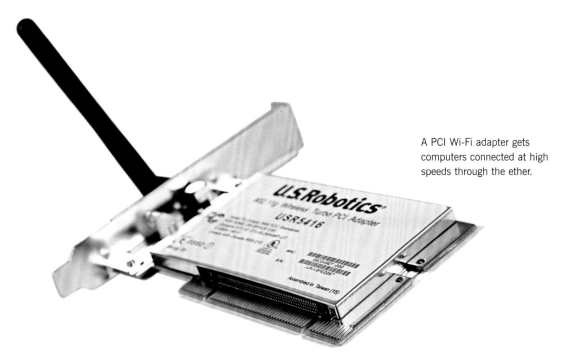

A PCI Wi-Fi adapter gets computers connected at high speeds through the ether.

Wireless networking (Wi-Fi)

If you want to connect PCs without running network cables around your home, install a Wi-Fi adapter. This is essentially Ethernet without wires. There are in fact three main Wi-Fi standards, known as 802.11a, b and g. The oldest of these, 802.11b, runs at a theoretical maximum speed of 11Mb/sec (about the same as the slowest version of Ethernet). This has since been largely replaced by 802.11g, which runs at 54Mb/sec. Hardware designed for either 802.11b or 802.11g will work together smoothly. 802.11a also runs at 54Mb/sec but is considerably less common and is not compatible with the other two standards.

Again, some motherboards provide built-in Wi-Fi.

FireWire (IEEE-1394)

FireWire is a high-speed (50MB/sec) interface particularly suited to transferring digital video from camcorder to computer or for connecting fast external drives. Need we say that FireWire is increasingly supported by motherboards?

It's an Apple trademark but FireWire works just as well on a PC as a Mac. If your motherboard comes up short, install a PCI expansion card.

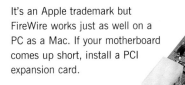

Killing two birds with one stone: a multi-format memory card reader plus floppy drive.

Media card reader

If you have a digital camera or a PDA (Personal Digital Assistant, or handheld computer), chances are it stores images and other files on a removable memory card. To transfer these files to your PC for editing, you can either connect the device with a cable – usually USB – or else plug the memory card into a card reader. You can get external card reading hardware, which is cumbersome, or internal models, which are convenient – particularly if it doubles-up as a floppy drive.

And the rest ...

A mouse, keyboard and monitor are definite givens, and a printer and scanner are obvious peripherals. But how else might you augment your PC?

Headphones and microphone Listen to music or games and record your own voice – or anything else – with a microphone. Windows has a sound recorder built-in but your sound card's software is likely to be more advanced. For use with speech recognition software, the best bet is a quality headset with an earpiece and microphone combined.

Joystick or games controller. These usually connect via a USB port but you can also get cordless models for greater flexibility.

Games controllers come in all shapes and sizes, from a simple joystick to this (whatever it may be).

USB hub Need more USB ports? A hub can add four or more with ease. You can get standalone external boxes or drive-mounted hubs that provide extra ports on the front of your computer.

This PCI expansion card provides SATA sockets for additional hard drives.

IDE or SATA controller card Add extra channels to your motherboard and connect another couple of hard disk drives. Essential for RAID, unless your motherboard provides native RAID support, and handy for massive storage requirements.

UPS (Uninterruptible Power Supply) Protect your files from power cuts with a UPS. Basically, it's a mini-generator that kicks in when the lights go out.

If the lights go out unexpectedly, will your data go with them? Not if you invest in a UPS.

Bluetooth A Bluetooth adapter lets your computer 'talk' to and exchange files wirelessly with other Bluetooth-enabled devices, notably mobile phones and PDAs.

CHOOSING YOUR HARDWARE

The perfect PC

We're going to build two computers from scratch: one that uses bang up-to-date components in a standard tower case and a tiny PC for home entertainment.

Making choices

The basic decision-making process looks like this:

- **Pick your processor** A Core 2 Duo or Athlon 64 X2 packs a lot of power, but a Pentium 4, Celeron D or AMD Sempron is much cheaper if you don't need impressive performance.
- **Choose your memory** DDR2 is usually your best bet and the more the merrier: if you want to take advantage of Windows Vista's various goodies, 1GB is a sensible amount and 2GB is even better. Windows XP is quite happy with around 512MB of RAM, although video editing and cutting-edge gaming needs 1GB.
- **Integrated multimedia** Do you want integrated sound and graphics or would you rather go for separate expansion cards? Integrated solutions keep the price down but, again, they impact on performance.
- **Choose the form factor** ATX and a tower case will do nicely in most circumstances, but of course we're also going to build a cute computer that uses a much smaller form factor.

Once you've settled these issues, the next step is to find a good motherboard with a chipset that provides all the right features. The main factors to consider, check, double-check and check again are:

- **Processor support** What socket does the motherboard have? What processor clock speeds does it support? What is the top FSB speed? If you're going for an older processor, will you be able to upgrade it later without replacing the motherboard too?
- **Memory support** What type of RAM does the motherboard need and how fast can it run? How much memory can you install? Are there any important restrictions?
- **Multimedia** Is there a 16x-speed PCI Express slot for a modern graphics card? If the motherboard has integrated graphics and you intend to stick with that for now, is there a spare PCI Express slot for future upgrades? If the motherboard has an integrated sound system, does it deliver surround sound or plain old stereo?
- **Hard disk support** Does the motherboard support IDE/ATA or Serial ATA? Both would be ideal.
- **Inputs and outputs** How many PCI expansion slots does the motherboard provide? Are there sufficient USB sockets? Do you need integrated networking or wireless networking?
- **Form factor** Will the motherboard fit in the case? ATX motherboards fit happily in ATX cases, but for smaller form factors you'll need a smaller motherboard too, such as a MicroATX model.

Our chipset choices

For our main PC, we've decided to build a high-end and very expandable PC based around a Core 2 Duo processor. It needs to be fast enough to edit video (and with storage capacity to match

– video files are massive) but not so loud that it deafens us when we're running. We went for Core 2 Duo because our preferred motherboard has an Intel chipset that supports DDR2 RAM, Serial ATA and PCI Express, although an AMD Athlon 64 X2 would have worked just as well.

Our choice is a Gigabyte motherboard (the GA 965P DS3) based on the Intel P965 Express chipset, which can cope not just with the hardware we're adding today but which has plenty of room for expansion in the future. We are not recommending Gigabyte over other motherboard manufacturers, though – it just happened to be the best board in our price range for the things we wanted to do.

The perfect PC, mark 1

Choosing the motherboard is the tricky bit; once you've got it, everything else is easy. Here's what we ended up with.

Component	Manufacturer	Model/specification	Notes
Motherboard	Gigabyte	GA 965P DS3	A standard ATX motherboard, so it should fit in our ATX case. It includes integrated audio delivering eight channels of surround sound and it supports both the latest processors and the latest memory technology.
Processor	Intel	Core 2 Duo E6700	This dual-core processor is right in the middle of the current Intel range, running at 2.67GHz, and it's very, very quick. If money's tight the motherboard also supports Pentium 4 CPUs.
Case	Akasa	AK-ZENO1-WH	A white midi-tower that's prettier than most, which has two internal fans and which promises to be quieter than the typical case. We actually wanted the black one, but it was out of stock everywhere we looked.
PSU	Akasa	AK-P050FG7-BKUK	This serious looking 500W power supply gives us lots of room to spare if we add hungry components in the future. Like the case, Akasa promises its PSU is quieter than most.
Memory	Crucial	BL2KIT12864AA80	These are two sticks of DDR2, 800MHz PC2-6400 RAM at 1GB apiece, the fastest kind of memory our chosen motherboard supports.
Hard disk	Samsung	HD400LJ	At 400GB the Samsung drive should have more than enough room for our home video files, even at high quality settings and, with a spin speed of 7,200RPM, it's quick too – which is essential for video.
Floppy disk	DabsValue	53-in-1 card reader	Floppies are dead but, thanks to digital cameras and mobile phones, memory cards are everywhere – so why not put a card reader in your floppy drive's place? That's what we're going to do.
DVD drive	LiteOn	SH-16A7S-053	A cheap, cheerful and very capable SATA DVD reader and burner that's compatible with all the major formats. We're steering clear of HD-DVD and Blu-Ray until a winner emerges.
Sound card	n/a	n/a	Included on motherboard.
Video card	Sapphire	11095-03-2DR	An extremely powerful bit of kit, and just what you need when you're working with video. This card is a Radeon X1950 Pro with a very respectable 512MB of RAM and a PCI Express interface. It has its own cooling fan and needs a direct connection to our PC's power supply.
TV Tuner	Hauppauge	WinTV Nova-T 500	This PCI card enables our PC to receive TV broadcasts, including Freeview ones. It's got twin tuners, which means we can record one programme while watching another, and it also supports digital radio.

The perfect PC Mark II

For our second project, we wanted to build a home entertainment-style PC based on an Athlon 64 processor. This proved easier said than done, as at the time of writing there was only one Athlon-compatible small form factor (SFF) motherboard available. However, this came in the welcome shape of a Shuttle barebones system.

The idea behind barebones kits is that you get much of the hardware you need in a single box. It's certainly convenient but it's also essential, as SFF kits tend to use non-standard motherboards, proprietary PSUs and custom cooling systems. All you have to do is buy a compatible processor, a couple of memory modules and a drive or two. The model we selected has integrated audio, USB and FireWire and gigabit Ethernet. However, a glance at its diminutive size tells you that there's not a great deal of room for drives or expansion. Here's the full specification:

Feature	Specification
Form factor	Proprietary design for the Shuttle FN95 motherboard
Chipset	nVidia nForce 3 Ultra
Processor interface	Socket 939 for Athlon 64
HyperTransport (MHz)	1,000
Memory interface	2 x DDR DIMMs with dual-channel support
Memory support	PC2100 DDR-266/PC2700 DDR-333/PC3200 DDR-400
Maximum memory	2GB
Video interface	AGP 8x-speed
Integrated audio	Realtek ALC655 codec with 5.1 support
Sound ports	Front channel out, rear channel out, centre/subwoofer channel out, line in, line out, mic in, coaxial SPDIF out, optical SPDIF in, optical SPDIF out
Expansion slots	1 x PCI
HDD interface	2 x IDE/ATA-133, 2 x SATA I
Floppy controller	Supports 1.44MB drive
Inputs/outputs	2 x PS/2 ports
USB 2.0	4 x ports (2 front, 2 rear)
FireWire	2 x ports (1 front, 1 rear)
LAN	Gigabit Ethernet
Wi-Fi	No
Modem	No
BIOS	Award

With so many features included and so little room for expansion, our shopping list for this PC was much reduced. Here are the details.

Component	Manufacturer	Model/specifications	Notes
Barebones kit	Shuttle	SN95G5 XPC	The kit comes with a Socket 939 motherboard that's compatible with Athlon 64 and 64 FX processors. The case is aluminium and comes with a proprietary 240W PSU.
Processor	AMD	Athlon 64 FX 3500+. No need for a heatsink because the Shuttle kit has its own cooling system.	We couldn't resist the FX version with its extra chunk of cache.
Memory	Kingston Technology	2 x 512MB PC-3200 DDR-400 modules (part number KVR400X64C3AK2/512)	These will be installed in a dual-channel configuration to provide 1GB of RAM running at effectively double the normal bandwidth. We chose the fastest memory that the motherboard chipset supports, but not its maximum complement of 2GB.
Hard disk drive	Seagate	1 x Barracuda 120GB (7,200rpm)	As with the Pentium 4 system earlier.
Floppy disk drive	Mitsumi	7-in-1 memory card reader and floppy drive	Also as before.
DVD drive	Lite-On	Multi-format dual-layer DVD writer	And again.
Sound card	-	-	-
Video card	Creative Labs	3D Blaster Ti4200	The motherboard has an 8x-speed AGP slot so we installed an 8x-speed card.
Wi-Fi card	US Robotics	Wireless Turbo PCI Adapter	With no built-in wireless networking, installing a Wi-Fi card is a sound move. However, we could have gone for a USB 'dongle', which would have the advantage of leaving the sole PCI slot clear for a different type of expansion card, such as a TV tuner. A lack of space forces such choices.

All unpacked and raring to go.

PART 3

Putting together a dual-core PC

All set?	78
Installing the processor and heatsink	80
Installing RAM	86
Installing the motherboard	88
Installing the power supply unit	94
Installing the DVD drive, card reader and hard disk	96
Installing the video card	102

Now, it's time to start building your computer – or in our case, computers. In this part, we'll build a dual-core desktop PC and, in Part 4, we'll create a tiny media PC for the living room. Although it's perfectly possible to build your entire computer in a few hours, you might prefer to start and stop at strategic intervals – so we've broken down the construction process into sensible sessions.

All set?

Just time for a couple of last-minute checklists.

Tooling up

There's no need to equip a workshop with expensive gadgets to build a computer. Here is a full and comprehensive list of all you will need.

- **Antistatic mat and wrist-strap** Electrostatic discharge (ESD) can do serious damage to motherboards and expansion cards, so protect your investment. At a minimum, we strongly recommend that you wear an antistatic wrist-strap whenever handling components. This should be clipped onto an unpainted bare metal part of the computer case. Better still, use an antistatic mat as well. In this case, you connect the wrist-strap cable to the mat and then connect the mat itself to the case. A component should be left safely ensconced within the antistatic bag it came in until you are ready to use it, and then rested on the antistatic mat before installation. Always – and we mean always! – unplug the power cable from the computer before commencing work.

Not a soldering iron in sight. You don't need a degree in electronics to fill a computer case with components.

A case full of computer tools is a clear case of overkill for the hobbyist system builder.

- **Screwdrivers** A couple of Phillips and flat-head screwdrivers will suffice.
- **Pliers** Get hold of a pair of plastic pointy pliers or other pick-up implement for setting jumpers and retrieving dropped screws.
- **Air duster** A can of compressed air is more of an ongoing maintenance tool than a construction aid, to be honest, but is useful for de-fluffing and unclogging second-hand components.
- **Adequate lighting** An Anglepoise or similar light is really useful. Ample daylight is a bonus and a small clip-on torch essential.
- **Patience** Tricky to illustrate on the page but an essential component in any successful PC project. It's best to accept from the outset that not everything will run entirely smoothly. We can guarantee that you will drop the odd screw inside the case, for instance, and it's a fair bet that you will hesitate when required to insert a memory module or heatsink with rather more force than seems reasonable. There's also a chance that something relatively minor – a forgotten cable here, a wrongly set jumper there, a loose connection anywhere – will set you back awhile and force a bout of fraught troubleshooting. But throughout the entire procedure, stay relaxed and think logically. Short of a hardware failure in a specific component, which is itself easily diagnosed, rest assured that your efforts will be rewarded.

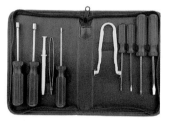

Ready-made screwdriver/pointy-thing kits like this one from Belkin are ideal.

PART 3 Installing the processor and heatsink

Putting the processor in place and attaching the heatsink is very straightforward, but it can also be a bit fiddly – so we think it's easier to do this step before you screw the motherboard into your PC case.

For this step, we'd strongly recommend using an antistatic mat and an antistatic wrist-strap to get rid of any static charge that might be hanging around your body, as such charges can be fatal to PC components. The instructions that come with the antistatic kit will explain how you can make sure it's properly earthed, and it's important to follow those instructions again to re-earth everything if you take a break and return to your PC project later. You don't need to be wearing a nylon shell suit and dancing around in deep pile carpet to build up enough static to fry an expensive component, and most hardware firms' warranties are null and void if you don't take adequate protection and accidentally zap something expensive.

Some motherboards have a removable tray that you screw the motherboard to; if your case is one of them, then you should take that out of the case now and attach the motherboard to it before continuing. For standard PC cases, though, you can start with this section.

1

Unpack the motherboard and hold it gently by the edges, taking care not to touch any of its components: some of them are fairly fragile and it's all too easy for careless fingers to knock something important out of action. Place the motherboard on a flat, clean surface (or on your antistatic mat, if you have one). Occasionally you'll find that the motherboard manufacturer has stuck a sticker across some of the slots, which is the case here. Very gently, prise the sticker off the expansion slots and curse the genius who thought pulling stickers on sensitive components was a smart thing to do.

2

Try to avoid leaving any residue from the sticker on the expansion slots, because it's a pain to get rid of. If there is some residue left when you've removed the sticker, gently scrape it off and make sure none of it falls inside the expansion slots themselves.

3

Locate the processor socket – if you have the motherboard facing towards you with its various input and output ports furthest away from you, the socket will be towards the right side of the motherboard. This is an Intel motherboard and the processor goes into a Socket 775 slot. The socket is protected with a metal cover and locked with a lever, so the first step is to unclip the lever and lift it up.

4

The socket cover is hinged at the back and should lift up easily. Be very gentle with the cover, as its hinges are easily damaged. Leave the cover up for now.

5

Once you've unlocked the processor, you should be able to remove the plastic protector. It's worth keeping hold of this: you'll need to put it back in if your motherboard turns out to be faulty and has to be returned to the manufacturer.

6

Holding your processor by the outside edges, look for the little gold triangle in one corner. There should be an accompanying indicator in the processor socket. Carefully line up the processor and gently lower it into place. Be extremely careful as you do this.

7

The processor should simply drop into position, and you'll know instantly whether it's been lined up correctly: if it has, a gentle press will make it sit securely in its socket and if it hasn't, it won't. You don't need to apply anything more than the lightest pressure to sit the processor in its socket and doing so would be a bad idea anyway: it'd bend the processor's pins, causing irreversible damage to it, to your motherboard or to both.

8 When you're confident that the processor is sitting happily in its socket, close the metal cover on top of it and use the lever to lock everything in place. The lever needs a bit of a push in order to close it. Remember to lock the lever in position by pushing it underneath the clip at the side of the processor socket.

9 And here's the result: one shiny new processor locked into its socket. You could connect the power at this point, but if you did the processor would immediately overheat and fry itself. Modern processors run at very high temperatures, so we'll need to fit a heatsink to keep it cool before we can do anything else. Provided you bought a retail processor and not a cheap, unpackaged OEM unit, the heatsink will be in the same box your processor came in. If you've bought an OEM chip, you'll need a separate heatsink and thermal paste to glue it to your processor.

This is our heatsink, and it's even heavier than it looks. The three stripes you can see on the bottom are the thermal paste that glues the heatsink to the top of your processor, and it's very important that you don't touch them or allow anything to touch them. When you handle the heatsink, hold it by its outside edges.

The heatsink has four 'legs', which are pins that fit into holes in your motherboard. Lift the heatsink over the processor socket and you should be able to see the appropriate holes. Gently lower the heatsink so each leg is in one of the holes.

Now for the scary bit. The manual says that you can now click the pins into place, but by click it means 'a horrendous cracking sound that makes you think you've snapped the motherboard'. The amount of pressure you need to use on each pin is truly frightening, but provided the motherboard is supported properly and can't bend, you'll be OK.

You'll know the pins have been inserted properly when you've heard four heart-stopping cracks as you push them into place and the heatsink doesn't move if you poke its legs. Under no circumstances attempt to move, let alone boot, your PC if the heatsink is not locked firmly into position. Doing so is a recipe for disaster.

13

You'll have noticed that the heatsink also includes a rather large fan, and you should never, ever, ever power up your PC if that isn't connected – doing so is a one-way ticket to meltdown city. The fan has a connector block attached to it, and this goes into the CPU_FAN socket on the motherboard – it's usually an inch or two away from the heatsink itself, on the very edge of the motherboard.

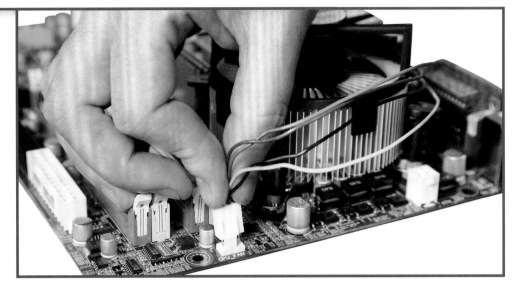

14

The heatsink's power cable is usually wrapped around the heatsink itself, and you might need to unwrap it a little bit so it reaches the motherboard connector. Just make sure that you don't unwrap it so much that the cable's likely to be hit by the fan blades as they spin or become snagged in other parts of the motherboard. Similarly, don't keep it so tightly wrapped that it bends the power connector on the motherboard. If that cable dies, your PC fries. Not a cheery thought.

PART ③ Installing RAM

Before we put the motherboard into our PC's case, we can install the memory modules: as with the processor, it's a little bit fiddly and it's much easier to do when the motherboard is sitting on a desk.

If your motherboard supports dual channel memory and you want to take advantage of it (which you should, because it delivers a significant performance boost), it's essential that your two or four RAM modules are identical. That means they need to run at the same speed and same capacity, and ideally they should come from the same manufacturer.

1

Once your heart's recovered from locking the heatsink into place, it's time to insert your memory chips. Depending on the kind of motherboard and kind of memory you've chosen, the number and size of the memory banks may differ from what you see here, but the principle is just the same.

As you can see, our RAM sockets are colour coded: two of them are red and two of them are yellow. That colour coding helps you see where to put your chips, because if you're putting in a pair of RAM modules they need to go in specific slots to enable dual-channel performance. In the case of our motherboard, that means if you put the first RAM module in a yellow socket then you need to put the second one in a yellow socket too. Consult your motherboard manual to see which sockets you need to use for your memory – putting the modules in the wrong sockets does make a difference, so it's better to get it right first time. In the case of our motherboard, the manual says we should use the top, yellow socket first and then the second yellow socket for our second memory module.

To insert a RAM module, open the clips on either edge of the socket and then line up the module with the slot. Memory is shaped and will only fit one way, so gently push the module into the socket and make sure its pins line up properly. If they don't, lift it out, turn it back to front and try again.

Time for another scary bit: to secure the RAM modules in place you'll need to apply a reasonable bit of force, because the sockets are a tight fit (deliberately so – you don't want the memory to fall out again if you move your PC).

Before you start shoving, make sure the module isn't round the wrong way – if it is, applying force could break the modules or your motherboard – and then apply pressure to each side of the module simultaneously. The module should now slide into place and the clips on the edges of the socket should lock automatically. If they don't, lock them manually with a quick flick of the finger.

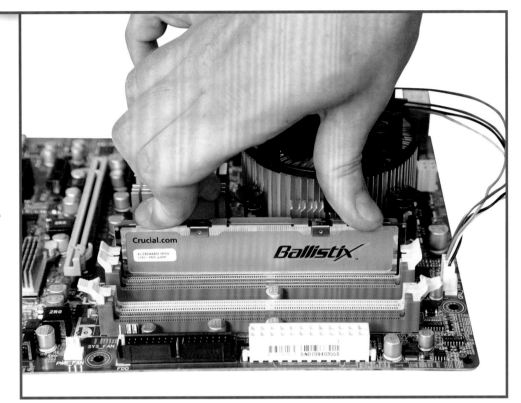

If you have a second memory module, the installation process is identical: line up the module, give it a good shove and lock it in place.

PART

Installing the motherboard

That's the scary stuff over with, so now we can put our motherboard into our PC. Things can get a little bit cluttered when you start adding disk drives, video cards and so on but, as we'll discover, it's all nice and simple.

If your computer case has a removable motherboard tray, you should attach the motherboard to it before doing anything else – and you'll be able to skip Step 4, where we screw little brass standoffs into the PC case.

QUICK Q&A

My motherboard doesn't fit!
Provided you've bought the right kind of motherboard – an ATX board to fit in an ATX case – then, while you might have difficulty lining up the various screws, it's unlikely that you've bought the wrong motherboard. It's much more likely that minor manufacturing errors mean that some holes are very, very slightly out of alignment. It's worth persevering: we've installed stacks of motherboards and we've yet to be beaten by one!

1

First things first: it's time to get the sides off the PC case so we can start sticking things into it. Different cases have different approaches; for example, some of them have fixing screws on the back that you'll need to unscrew with a star screwdriver, others have thumbscrews that you can loosen and remove by hand, and really fancy cases have a magic lever that you pull to unlock the case sides. The method doesn't matter: what does matter is that you get the sides off. We've only taken one side off, but you'll need to remove both in order to secure your hard disks and other peripherals.

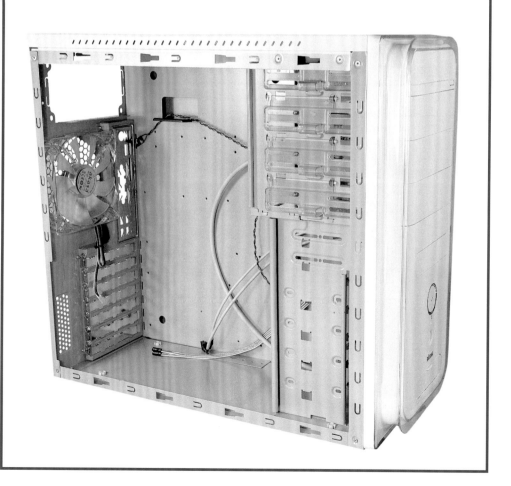

②

Turn the case around so you're looking at the back and you should see a blanking plate with spaces for connectors such as the keyboard, the mouse, the USB ports and so on. It's nice that it's there, but unfortunately the chances are that it's completely useless because it won't even vaguely match the connectors on the back of your motherboard. That means it needs to come out – and even more unfortunately, the only way to do that is to grab it with your fingers and give it a good yank. As the blanking plate is made of very thin metal, be very careful here or you'll end up giving yourself a cut.

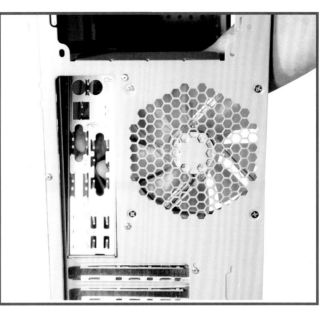

③

The packaging of your motherboard should include a spanking new blanking plate for the back of your PC case, and it's just a matter of putting it into place and pushing it until it snaps in. Again, watch your fingers. Make sure it's the right way up – in this photo, the top of the case is to the right – and be careful when you put it in place as the thin metal is all too easy to bend.

④

We're nearly ready to install the motherboard, but first we need to lay the case on its side so we can get easy access to its innards. When you've done that you'll see that there's a metal sheet inside the case for your motherboard to sit on, and it's got lots of little holes in it. The holes are for standoffs, little brass stands that screw into the tray and which you then screw the motherboard to, and you'll find dozens of them in a little bag that came with your motherboard.

You don't need to put a standoff in every available hole, but you do need to put one in each hole that corresponds to a hole in your motherboard. The smart thing to do, then, is to hold the motherboard over the tray, identify which holes you need, and then screw in the appropriate standoffs. Don't be tempted to skip this step, no matter how dull it seems: it's essential that your motherboard is properly affixed to the case.

5

Once you've attached your bits of brass, it's time to put the motherboard in position. The easiest way to do this is to start from the back of your case by lining up its various ports and connectors with the blanking plate you just fitted. Once you've done this, gently lower the motherboard onto the brass standoffs.

6

As you'd expect, once the motherboard's in the right position you need to screw it into place. Again, the screws you need will be in a little bag that came with your motherboard. Don't be entirely surprised if you drop a screw doing this, because it's very fiddly – but don't use a magnetic screwdriver to fish it out or leave the screw inside your PC case forever.

Depending on the kind of case you've bought it will have one, two or even three fans to keep everything nice and cool. Although the connectors aren't marked they're easy enough to identify by simply finding the cables that snake from the fans. To connect a fan, plug its connector block into an appropriate space on the motherboard. There are several, marked SYS_FAN, PWR_FAN and so on.

If you have more than one case fan, you'll need to connect that too. The procedure is identical, but make sure you don't use the connection marked CPU_FAN – you should already have the heatsink plugged into that one!

9

In addition to its fans, your case has a bunch of connectors for the power button, the drive activity LED and so on. Although these connectors are marked, there's no clue as to which way round they should go – and it's the same on the motherboard, which tells you where to connect them but doesn't say which way round they need to go. Here, we've connected our various front panel cables and we're hoping they're all round the right way. In some cases it doesn't matter, but if any of the front panel features such as the reset button or LED doesn't work then it means you've got the connector back to front and you'll need to swap it round. It's easily one of the most annoying things about PC building.

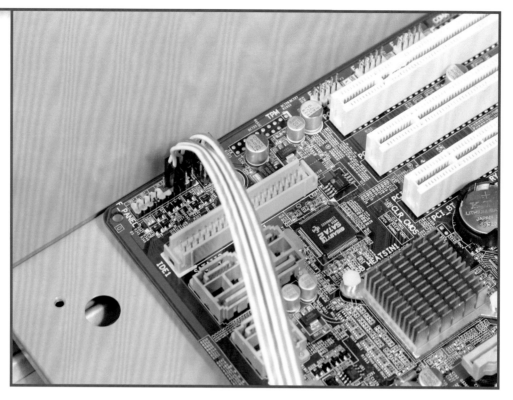

More case connectors? We're afraid so. This time we need to connect the front audio panel, which provides handy access to the headphone and microphone socket. This one's nice and easy: on the motherboard you'll see a connector marked F_AUDIO, and that's the one you need to use.

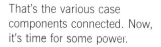

Most cases also have front-mounted USB ports which, once again, are very handy. And once again, they need to be connected to the motherboard. As with the audio connector, the appropriate motherboard sockets are easy enough to find, and they're helpfully marked with the legend USB.

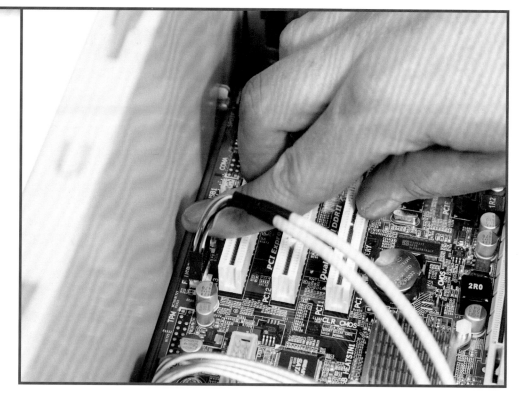

If you've got more than one front USB port you'll have more than one cable to connect. The second USB connector on your motherboard should be right next to the first one.

That's the various case components connected. Now, it's time for some power.

Installing the power supply unit

If your case came with a power supply unit preinstalled, then great. In most cases, though, you need to provide your own power supply unit. With smaller cases, if the PSU is already installed, you may need to remove it temporarily before you can fit the motherboard.

Once everything's connected, it's a good idea to connect the power cable to the power supply, plug the cable into the wall, press the switch on the back of the power supply unit to the On position and switch on the PC to make sure it's working (although of course you need to steer well clear from the insides – you don't want to electrocute yourself). If everything's connected properly, you should see the various fans spinning, including the one on the heatsink.

If your motherboard doesn't have integrated graphics (because you've done the same as we did and invested in a stand-alone video card) and you leave the PC running, you'll almost certainly hear a number of beeps after a few seconds. The beeps are giving you a fault code, which you can use to diagnose hardware problems.

If you're wondering why your PC beeps instead of just telling you what the problem is with an on-screen error message, it's because beeps are like the cockroaches of the computing world: they can survive almost anything. Provided your motherboard has power and you remembered to connect your PC speaker, your PC can make beeping noises even when other major components – the processor, the memory or the video card – aren't functioning. An on-screen message telling you your video card's not working is useless, because if your video card's broken or hasn't been connected correctly then you won't be able to see it.

Back to business. As we already know what the hardware problem is – we haven't put a video card into our PC just yet, so our PC is saying, 'Beep! No video card! Beep!' – there's no need to worry, but if you want to make doubly sure then refer to p.158 for our explanation of beep codes and what they're trying to tell you.

Before continuing, make sure you disconnect the power cable and switch everything off again. Never work on a PC that's plugged into the mains, even if the PC itself is switched off. Until you unplug the power cable, there's still enough electricity inside your PC to seriously ruin your day – so always double-check that you've disconnected the power before going anywhere near your PC's insides. Remember to re-earth your antistatic protection too. You can't be too careful.

Installing a power supply is nice and simple, although actually screwing it into place is a little tricky – and isn't helped by the fact that power supply units are much heavier than they appear. If your case has a shelf for the power supply to sit on – most do – you'll need to press it against that while simultaneously lining up the power supply unit's screw holes with the pre-drilled holes in your PC case. Once you've done that, you can screw the power supply into place. Make sure it's nice and tight because, if it isn't, your PC will quickly develop a really annoying rattle, but don't overtighten the screws or you may strip their threads, in which case they may work loose over time.

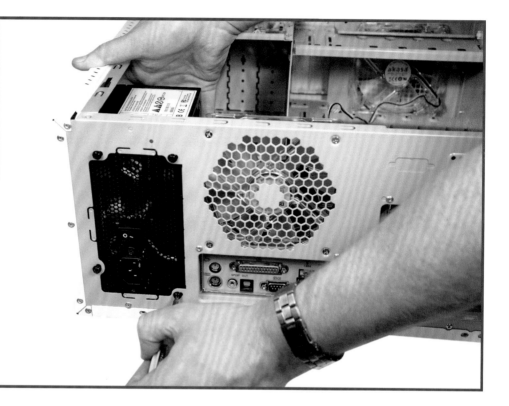

Once the power supply unit is in place, connect the motherboard power block to the appropriate socket on the motherboard. You can't miss it – it's a huge socket along the edge of the motherboard nearest the power supply unit, and the connector block is shaped so you can't put it in the wrong way round. Our motherboard takes the standard 24-pin connector that our power supply unit's mess of cables includes, but your PSU should also include an adapter that enables you to connect older motherboards that have a slightly different 20-pin connector design. If you're using an older motherboard with an early Pentium 4 processor, look for the ATX 12V connection too (see p.50 for a picture).

PART

Installing the DVD drive, card reader and hard disk

Installing DVD drives and hard disks is very straightforward, especially if they use the modern Serial ATA (SATA) connectors. Because SATA devices use a special power plug, though, it's essential that your power supply unit has the necessary power connectors for your SATA drives.

If you're using older IDE/ATA drives you'll make connections with big ribbon cables instead of the slim SATA cables in our PC, but the principle is the same. However, there's one crucial difference with IDE/ATA drives: jumpers. If two drives are going to share the same IDE/ATA channel, you need to set one as the master and one as the slave. To do this, you need to fit a plug called a jumper to connect two little pins on the back of the drive. The drive manual should tell you which pins to connect for the master and which for the slave, and the packaging should also include the jumpers themselves. If you can't see the jumpers, check the back of the drives: they're often fitted before the drive leaves the factory.

Many cases now include plastic securing brackets for your 5.25 inch drives, which means you don't have to muck about with screws when you want to secure your drive in an empty bay. Our case is one of those models, but before we can put our DVD drive into a spare drive bay we need to open the securing brackets on both sides of the PC case. Unclipping the brackets is simple: it's just a matter of giving the tab a gentle squeeze and then lifting up the bracket.

②

Once you've unclipped the securing brackets, turn your attention to the front of the case and pop off the plastic cover that sits over the drive bay you want to use. The cover is usually secured by two plastic clips, and if you reach inside the case and give both clips a squeeze you can then pop the cover off by pushing it outwards. Once you've done that it's just a matter of sliding the DVD drive into the hole by pushing it gently into place. You might need to use your other hand to hold the securing clips out of the way as you do this.

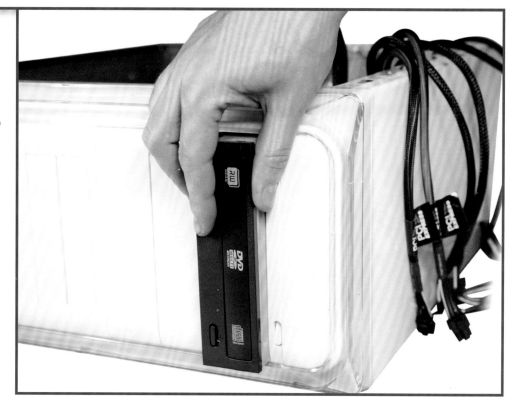

③

You'll see that on each side of the DVD drive there are screw holes. Line them up with the holes in the case itself and you should now be able to lock the securing clips in place by pushing them down until they lock. Don't push too hard – if the holes aren't lined up exactly with the pins in the securing bracket, trying to force the bracket to close will just break the pin. Gently move the drive around until the holes line up perfectly and the pin pops into place without any fuss – and remember to do the same with the bracket on the other side of the case.

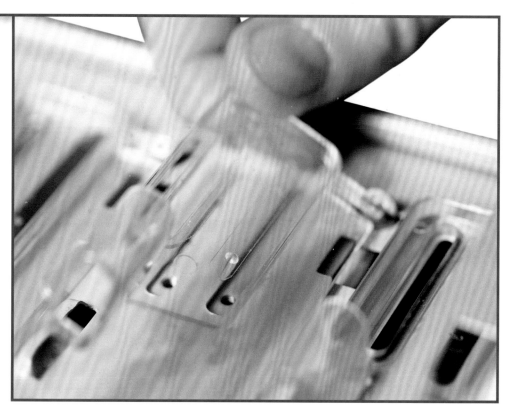

4

Installing the hard disk drive is essentially the same process as installing the DVD drive, but there are a few key differences. First, the hard disk is a 3.5 inch model, so we need to use one of the smaller drive bays further down the front of the case; secondly, there aren't any securing clips to worry about; and thirdly, you don't need to remove the front cover panel because you never need to see the front of your hard disk drive. Simply slide the hard disk drive into position and make sure its screw holes line up with the ones in the case's drive bay.

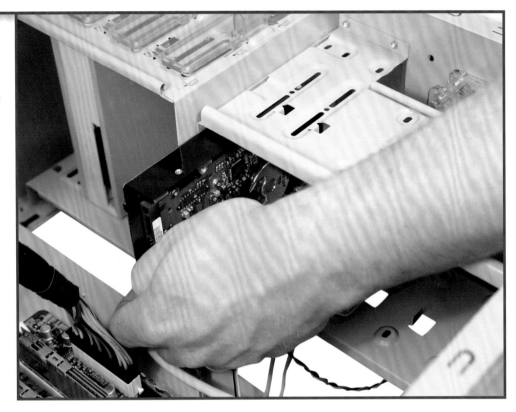

5

Because there aren't any securing brackets, we need to secure the hard disk drive using good old-fashioned screws, which should have come in a bag inside the hard disk packaging. Remember to put screws in both sides of the drive bay to avoid vibration and rattling.

6

Instead of a floppy disk drive, we'll install a multi-card reader, which sits in a spare drive bay. As with our DVD drive we need to unclip the securing clips, pop off the panel covering the drive bay and slide the card reader into place, but there's one important difference: it's a USB device, which means it needs to be plugged into a spare USB port – and those ports are outside the case. The answer's simple, though: there's a spare hole in the back of the case (it's designed for really old motherboards that have a serial port, which is a rarity these days), so we can pop its cover off and run the card reader's USB cable through that and connect it to one of the USB ports on the back of the PC.

7

Now we need to give our drives some power. Our power supply unit has a mass of cables coming from it with a range of different connectors. One of those cables is an SATA power cable with connectors for two SATA devices. By a happy coincidence, our DVD drive and our hard disk are both SATA devices, so we can use the same power cable for both. You'll see that the cable has two power connectors, one in the middle and one at the very end; plug the middle one into the power socket in the back of the DVD drive.

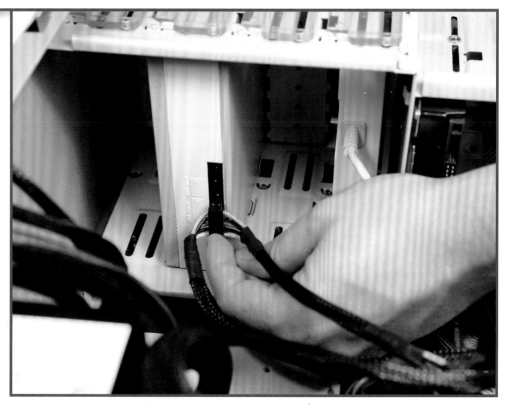

8

As you'd expect, the next step is to plug the connector at the end of the SATA power cable into the socket on the back of the hard disk drive. You've successfully added power to both of your drives. Now, it's time to add their data connections too.

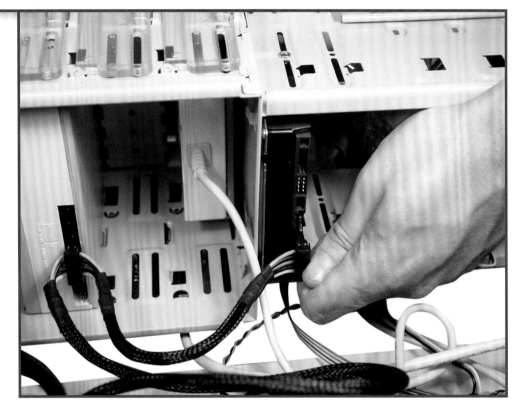

9

Your motherboard's packaging should include various extra cables and if, like ours, it supports SATA devices, those cables should include SATA data cables – which is handy, because we need them now. Take one of the cables and plug it into the SATA data socket in the back of the DVD drive. The cable is shaped so it can only be connected in one way. Now, take the second SATA data cable and connect it to the socket on the back of your hard disk.

Now, you need to plug the other ends of your SATA cables into the appropriate places on the motherboard. Take your first cable and look for the sockets marked SATA on the motherboard – on ours, they're near the front left corner of the motherboard and marked in bright colours. Once again the cables are shaped, so you can't connect them the wrong way round.

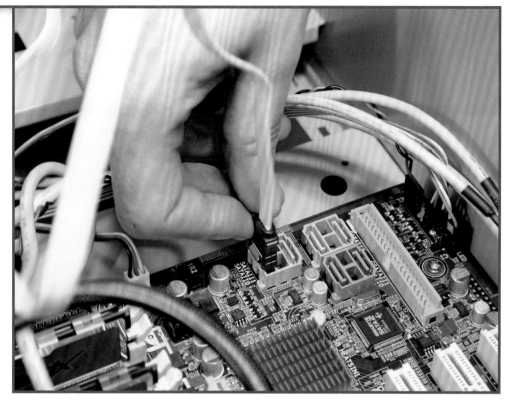

Repeat the process with the second SATA data cable. Your motherboard should now look like this, with twin SATA cables – one for the DVD drive, one for the hard disk – connected to the motherboard's SATA data connectors. It's worth checking the motherboard manual at this point because some older boards offer both high speed and slightly lower speed SATA connections, and you need to use the high-speed ones with the latest, fastest hard disks.

We're making excellent progress: we have a processor, we have RAM, we have power and we have storage. As the motherboard has its own integrated sound card, all that's left to do is add the video hardware. As we'll discover, that couldn't be simpler.

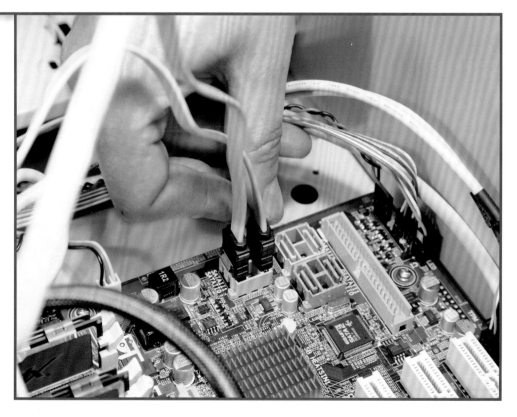

PART **3** # Installing the video card

Our PC is coming along nicely. We have a processor, we have power, we have memory and we have storage, so now it's time to add the video card. We'll also install a TV tuner card so we can use our PC as a digital video recorder.

The video card we've chosen is a PCI Express device and while it plugs into a spare slot like any other expansion card, it has a few unique things you need to watch out for. First of all, the tail – the end of the card furthest away from the back of the PC – needs to be locked in place, because such video cards are very heavy and would be unstable if they weren't locked into place. The same applies to AGP cards, the predecessor of PCI Express.

PCI Express cards also need a direct connection from the power supply, because the motherboard can't provide enough power for today's extremely demanding video technology.

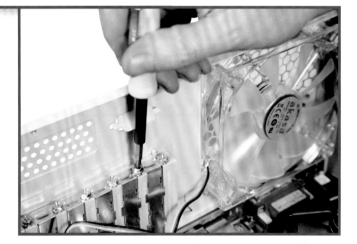

Before you can install your video card, you need to make room for it. Every PC case has a selection of PCI slots, which are spaces for add-in cards such as video cards, but by default the places they go are covered up with metal plates to stop dust getting into the system. Before we can install our graphics card, then, we need to remove the plate that corresponds to the slot we're going to put our card in – in this case, the PCI Express slot, which is second from the right. To remove the plate, simply remove the single screw holding it in place (with some PC cases there's a clip instead of screws; just lift up the clip) and then remove the metal plate.

Remember how you had to apply a fair bit of force to insert your memory modules? It's the same with graphics cards. Check that the card's pins are lined up with the slot and then press down firmly to lock it into place. Once the card is in its correct position use the screw or clip that held the blanking plate in place to secure the video card.

❸

If, like us, you've gone for a PCI Express graphics card, it needs its own power supply and won't work without one. On this Sapphire card, like most PCI Express cards, the power socket is at the end nearest you (if you're looking at it from the front of the PC). Locate the appropriate cable running from the power supply unit and connect it to the graphics card's power socket.

❹

In addition to our graphics card we'll also install a TV tuner card that enables our PC to receive TV broadcasts and act as a digital video recorder. As it's a standard PCI card, we don't need to connect a dedicated power supply but, as with our graphics card, we need to remove a blanking plate from the back of the PC, push the card into a spare slot and then use the screw or clip to anchor it in place.

Congratulations – you've built an entire PC. All that's left to do now is a bit of tidying up. If your power supply unit came with cable ties (most do) it's a good idea to use them to keep spare cables out of the way and to ensure that no cables get too close to whirring fans or hot bits such as the processor's heatsink (see Part 5 for more details of this). Once you've done that, you can replace the sides of your PC case, connect the keyboard, mouse and monitor and enter the very last stage of PC building: installing the operating system.

 TECHIE CORNER

If your motherboard has onboard video and you plan to use it, you'll need to fit the VGA port bracket that came with your motherboard. The bracket includes a cable that plugs into the motherboard – the motherboard manual will tell you where to connect it – and it goes in place of one of the PCI blanking plates at the back of your PC.

If you decide to upgrade your graphics later on, you might need to disable the onboard graphics processor in your system BIOS. We say 'might' because many motherboards automatically disable onboard graphics when they detect a new graphics card. Your motherboard manual will tell you whether your particular board has this auto-detection feature or whether you'll need to fiddle with the BIOS.

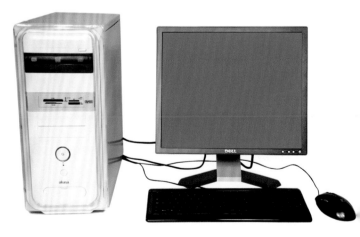

We're ready to roll: our PC is ready to run and it's time to install the operating system so we can start using it.

PART 4 Assembling an Athlon SFF PC

Upfront preparation	106
Fleshing out the barebones	108
Installing the drives	114
Installing the video and expansion cards	118

In the previous project, we could just as easily have used an AMD processor and virtually everything would have been identical save for a slightly altered processor and heatsink installation. But now it's time to build an altogether different PC. This time we will base it around an Athlon 64 FX chip.

PART 4 **Upfront preparation**

In the previous project, the motherboard and case came separately. But with a 'barebones' small form factor (SFF) kit such as the Shuttle SN95G5, the computer is already half-built. The motherboard and PSU are both pre-installed, so there's no need to fit standoffs or fiddle with the rear input/output panel and those awkward front panel connections. This makes assembly very much quicker. The only real downside is that your working space is much reduced.

Your first task with any barebones kit is to disassemble it. It's well worth making notes as you go along here or even snapping your own step-by-step photos with a digital camera, for it all has to go back together in exactly the same way. The exact routine obviously varies according to the model but the goal is the same: an empty box with just the motherboard and PSU remaining. Please note that you should leave the main PSU power cable connected to the motherboard throughout; or, if you find that it is not connected when you strip the case, plug it in at the outset.

The SN95G5 is a fairly typical cube-shaped SFF PC. This is what it looks like straight out of the box and also what it will look like when it's finished. But right now, our barebones kit has nothing much inside. Unscrew the thumbscrews on the rear to get inside.

②

Slide the single cover towards the rear and upwards to free it. Now lift it off completely and put it somewhere safe. If we mentioned that we once managed to sit on a flimsy SFF case cover, you'd only laugh – but it was no fun at the time.

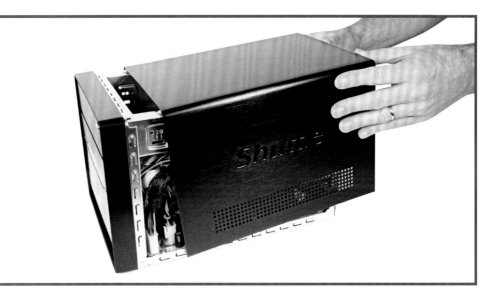

③

With space at such a premium inside this box, everything fits together very precisely indeed and there's not a wasted square centimetre. In fact, there's no way to access the motherboard unless you first remove the drive bay cage. This unscrews and lifts out completely.

④

You must also remove the cooling system. This is a proprietary design, seen here in isolation. The fan is attached to the vent on the rear of the case and connected to the heatsink by means of cooling pipes. The bracket is used to secure the heatsink to the processor socket. Note the power cable and remember to plug this into the motherboard later.

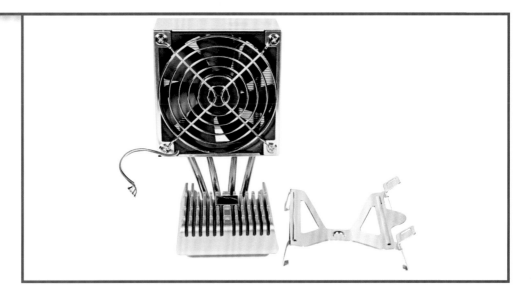

PART **4**

Fleshing out the barebones

We can't work with the motherboard outside the case here as we did on p.80–87 so be prepared for some nimble finger work. If you were installing an Athlon processor in a 'normal' tower-style PC, you would probably use the cooling system supplied with the processor. In that case, the installation procedure would be very similar indeed to the Pentium 4 routine. Here, there's simply no room for a standard heatsink or fan so it all gets a bit more complicated. But only a bit.

1

We can see the Socket 939 design for Athlon 64 and 64 FX on the Shuttle motherboard. It's basically similar to the Pentium 4 Socket 775 with one key difference: here, the socket has holes and the processor has the pins.

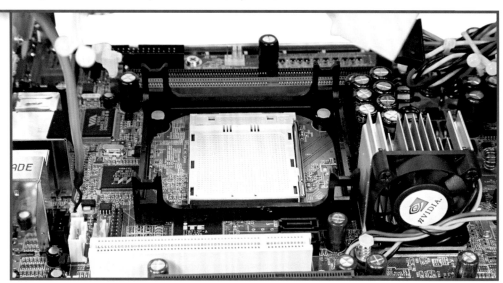

2

Lift the lever that runs adjacent to the socket to its fully upright position. This opens the pin holes and prepares the socket to receive the processor.

Handle your Athlon processor with great care. If you bend a pin, the damage is permanent. Look for the gold triangle in one corner (top-left here). This denotes the Pin 1 position. You must match this triangle to a similar marking on the processor slot.

Carefully lower the processor onto the socket, checking that the lever is still upright and that you have matched Pin 1 positions. The processor can only be installed in one orientation and the pins and pin holes should match perfectly.

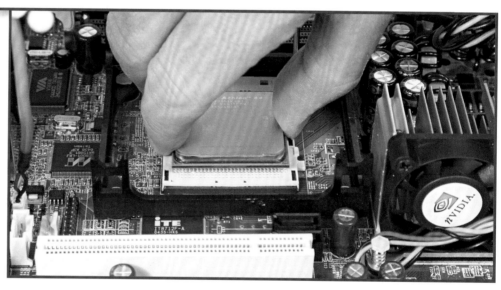

Gently press the processor home in the socket. It should lie completely flat and flush. If you have the slightest doubt, double-check that you are matching Pin 1 on the processor with Pin 1 on the socket. You can see the gold triangle marking on the upper side of the processor as well as on the pin side.

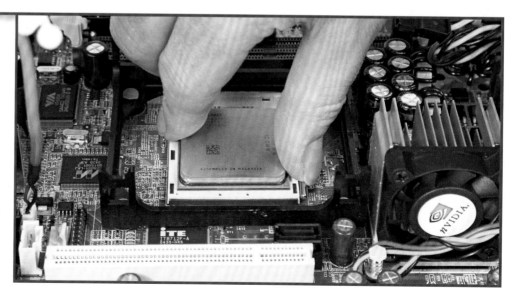

6

Back on p.82, our Pentium 4 cooling unit came with a pre-applied thermal interface, but our Shuttle cooling unit does not. Instead, it is supplied with a sachet of thermal glue. Squeeze the full amount onto the centre of the processor.

7

Spread it out more or less evenly over the square, silver part of the processor using a business card or something similar. The purpose of this glue is not to stick the cooling unit in place but rather to ensure the best possible conductive bond. Without it, the cooling unit would not be able to draw away sufficient heat from the processor.

8

Now for the tricky part. Lower the cooling unit onto the frame that surrounds the processor socket. The unit is attached to a fan with pipes and the fan goes to the rear of the case, so there's no room for doubt over which way it goes. However, try to get it right first time to avoid spreading the thermal gunk all over the place.

9

Press the heatsink firmly into the socket frame and onto the processor. Now place the retention frame over the heatsink. One side has an obvious tab, which we'll need in the next step. Meanwhile, hook the catches on the opposite sides into the holes in the raised arms of the socket frame.

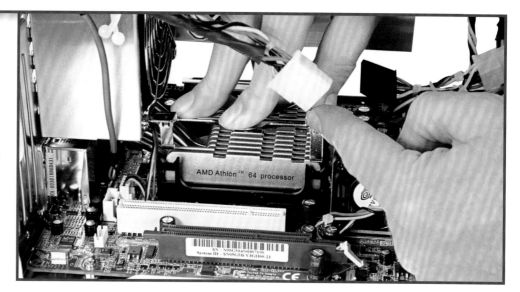

10

Carefully, but with a measure of brute force, press down on the retention frame tab to hook the remaining two catches into the retention frame's arms. You may need a few goes at this – we did, anyway – but that's okay so long as you don't overly disturb the heatsink.

11

Plug the cooling unit's power cable into the appropriate socket on the motherboard. In this example, it is clearly labelled and located conveniently close to the socket.

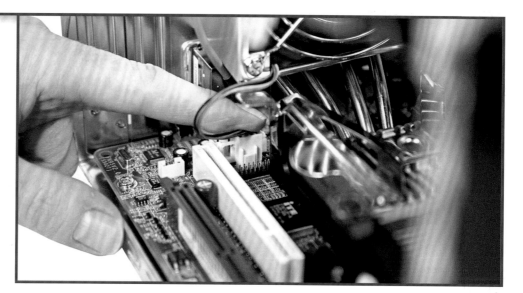

12

Now secure the fan section of the cooling unit to the grille on the rear of the case, using the four thumbscrews provided.

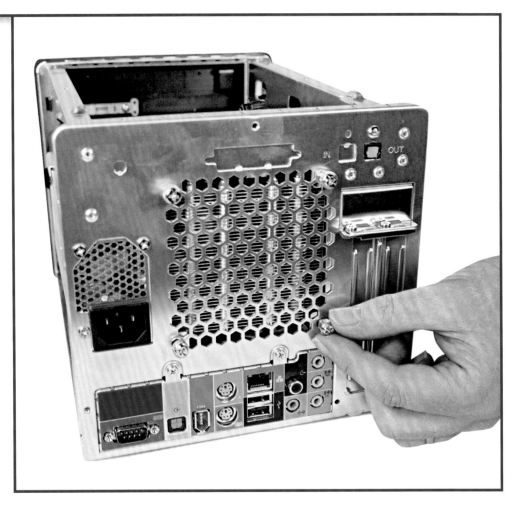

13

Looking down on the finished installation with the integrated power cables pulled out of the way, we can see the retention frame in place over the heatsink and the fan attached to the rear of the case (to the right here). That's the hard part over.

14

Let's move straight onto the memory installation. Just as on p.86–87, open the catches at either end of the first DIMM slot and carefully align your first memory module. Hold it vertical and match the notches on its lower edge with the notches in the slot. If you are installing a single module, use DIMM 1.

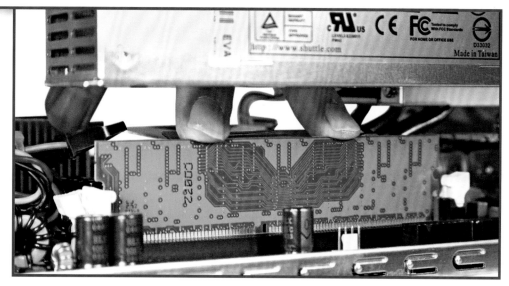

15

Press down firmly on the module to snap the slot catches shut. The module must be completely level in the slot. Again, it's all a bit cramped in here so take care.

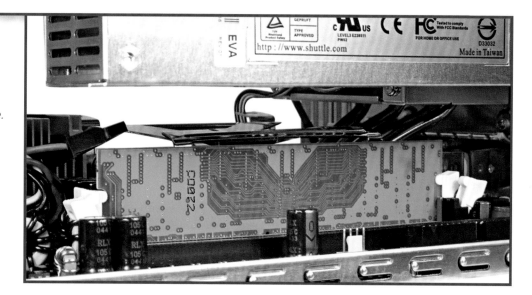

16

This Shuttle motherboard supports dual-channel memory (DDR only, not DDR2) so we'll install a second, identical module in DIMM 2. That's all that's required to double the memory bandwidth, for the chipset takes care of everything else automatically.

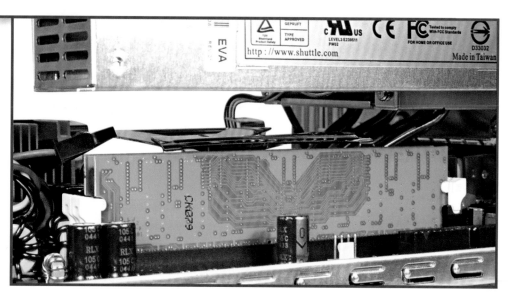

PART  # Installing the drives

Our SFF kit has room for one hard disk drive, one floppy drive (or, optionally, a second hard disk) and one optical drive. The installation procedure is quite different from that of a tower case but clever design makes it straightforward. Here we'll install three drives in one easy procedure.

1

In Step 3 on p.107, we removed the drive bay cage. The hard drive can now be screwed into this cage in the standard manner i.e. with four screws. Check how the cage fits within the case and be sure to install the drive so that its rear end – the end with the sockets – faces into the case.

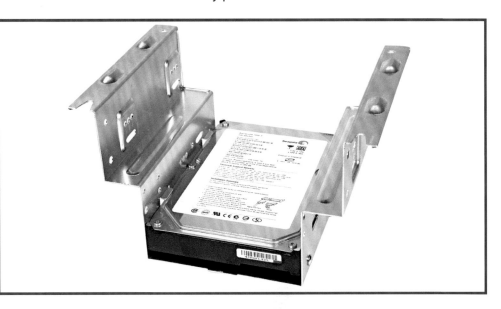

2

Now is the time to think about jumper configurations if you're using an IDE/ATA drive. Ours is SATA so these concerns don't apply. Slide the drive bay cage into the case with the drive in situ and reattach it with the screws you removed earlier.

You'll find that the power cable is routed around the side of the case from the PSU to just the right position. Connect this to the hard drive. Here it's a SATA-style power cable. Then connect the supplied data cable – again, we're dealing with SATA – to the drive.

Plug the other end of the data cable into the motherboard socket. Our motherboard has SATA and IDE/ATA sockets but we're only interested in the first SATA channel. The hard drive is now ready to run.

5

There's space above the hard disk drive for a floppy drive or a second hard disk drive. We'll plump for the same floppy/memory card reader drive you saw earlier. Slide the drive into place in the cage. It is possible to attach it to the cage at the same time as the hard drive (see Step 1), i.e. while the cage is outside the case. However, it's important to align the front of the drive with the drive opening on the case fascia and this is easier when the cage has already been installed.

6

When correctly aligned so that the front of the drive is flush with the fascia, screw the drive in place in the cage. Now connect the supplied (short) floppy drive cable to both drive and motherboard socket. Also connect the PSU power cable to the drive.

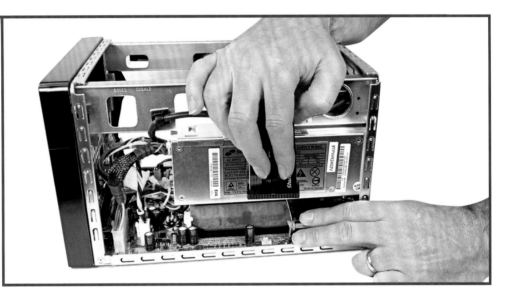

7

As this drive requires an internal USB connection to control the memory card reader, connect the drive's USB cable to a USB socket on the motherboard. Er, except that we discovered that we couldn't. This motherboard has two USB sockets but they are the wrong shape for our drive's plug. The result was that we couldn't use the drive as a memory card reader. If there's a lesson to be learned here, it's buy your motherboard (or barebones kit) first and study it before buying other components. Compatibility simply can't be taken for granted.

8

Slide your optical drive into the vacant 5.25-inch section of the drive bay cage but don't screw it in place just yet.

9

This case design keeps the optical drive hidden behind a panel. To access the drive, you press a small button on the front of the case. This is not an electrical operation but rather a mechanical lever that activates the tray-opening button on the drive. You may need to adjust the mechanism slightly in order to align the pressure pad on the lever with the drive's button. This sounds more complicated than it is.

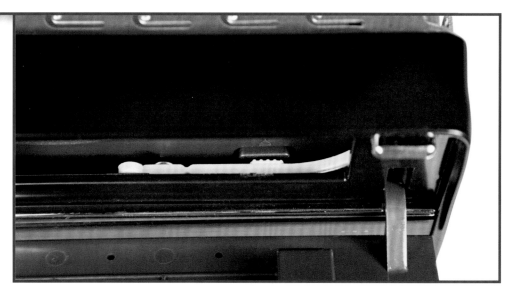

10

Connect the power and data cables to the drive and the data cable to the motherboard. Again, a special short data cable is provided. If you were using a SATA drive, you would use the second SATA motherboard channel. Finally, screw the optical drive to the drive cage.

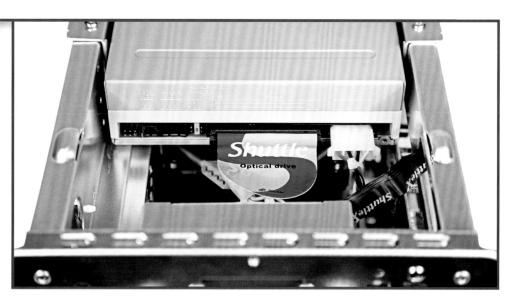

PART 4 Installing the video and expansion cards

This barebones kit has two slots: a fast AGP 8x-speed slot for a video card and a plain old-fashioned PCI card for anything else you fancy. But only one of anything you fancy, mind. We'll install a Wi-Fi card but you may prefer a TV tuner card, particularly if you want to run Windows Media Center or similar on your PC.

1

This Shuttle case has a catch mechanism for securing expansion cards. Lift this and remove the two blanking plates. Now install the PCI card in the PCI slot. Our Wi-Fi card has an aerial on its faceplate so extra care is required.

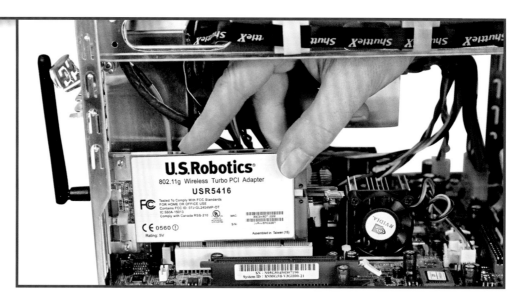

2

Install the video card next. Because this is a high-speed AGP card, it has a tail that must be secured in the slot with a retention clip. Note that we have customised this card by removing its original cooling unit and fitting a silent fan-free heatsink in its place. See Step 4 for more on this.

3 Close the expansion card catch and screw it in place. This secures the two cards in place.

4 As you can see from this angle, the video card's silent heatsink comes perilously close to the edge of the case and looks like it will only just clear the cover. The fact is that some cards have such bulky cooling units that they simply don't fit. For instance, the video card we used in the Pentium 4 tower project earlier would be far too wide for this SFF case. It's well worth checking the support and user forum sections of the case or kit manufacturer's website for guidance as problematic cards may be known and flagged as such.

5 Make a final check of the internal connections, checking that the main power cable is still connected to the motherboard. Now, with the case cover back on and secured with thumbscrews, and with a power cable connected, our mini PC is effectively ready to go.

6 But first, just check that the optical drive release mechanism works (see Step 9 on p.117). With the power on, the drive tray should open when you press the silver button in the top-right corner. If the masking panel fails to flip open like this, adjust the release mechanism until it does.

5

PART **5** **Final touches**

Connecting a monitor and switching on	**122**
Essential system settings	**124**
Installing Windows Vista	**128**
Installing a sound card	**135**
Digital audio extraction	**137**
Loose ends	**138**
Free software	**140**
Troubleshooting	**146**

We told you it was easy. All that remains now is to set up the computer to behave to your liking, install an operating system and finish off with a final expansion card. We will cover trouble-shooting in some detail, too, just in case of problems.

PART **5** # Connecting a monitor and switching on

At this point in the proceedings, you might be tempted to rush into further installations: the sound card, perhaps, or an internal modem or network card. However, now is the time to establish that everything has gone according to plan so far. Adding extra components merely complicates trouble-shooting, should any be required.

With a monitor and keyboard connected, and optionally a mouse, give your new computer its first trial run.

Check it out

Give your work-in-progress a thorough once-over. Check that the heatsink and case fans are all still connected to the motherboard, that the memory modules are still clipped into their DIMMs, that the drives are all wired-up with ribbon and power cables, and that the video card is fully secured in its slot. You might like to reassemble the case now but it's not strictly necessary. You can even leave the case lying on its side to better monitor the action. However ... you will be working with live electricity from here on so never touch anything inside your PC's case while the PSU is connected to the mains power. Even when you turn off your computer, the PSU continues to draw power from the mains and the motherboard remains in a partially-powered standby state. We're only talking a 5V current, to be fair, but it's simply crazy to work on a 'live' motherboard or anything connected to it.

True, you could flip the PSU to Off (if it has its own power switch) and/or turn off the electricity at the wall socket (and hope that Junior doesn't turn it back on for a laugh while your head is buried in the case), but it's better and safer to get into the habit of always removing the power cable before conducting any internal work. This is the only cast-iron way to ensure no physical connection between yourself and the National Grid.

Booting up ... and down again

Connect the monitor to the video card's VGA or DVI port and plug it in to the mains. Turn on the monitor now. You might see a 'no signal' or similar message on the screen.

Now check that the PSU is set to the correct voltage – 220/230V in the UK – and connect it to the mains with your second power cable. Flip the PSU's power switch to the on position. Finally, press the on/off button on the front of the case. Your PC will come to life for the first time.

Look inside the case and check – by observation, not by touch – that the heatsink and case fans are whirring. If not, kill the mains power immediately and check the fan cable connections on the motherboard. Ignore any beeps for now.

All being well, power your computer down with the on/off button and unplug the power cable. Leave the power switch on the PSU at the on position from now on. If all is not well, skip to p.146 now for some troubleshooting procedures.

Let us now turn our attention to some important configuration settings.

Once you're sure all your components are connected, you can put your PC's case back together.

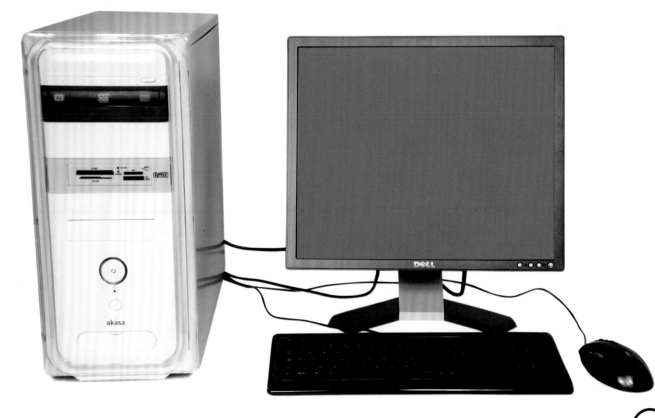

PART 5

Essential system settings

The hard work is over, and you're nearly ready to use your brand new PC. However, before you can do that you need to know about two acronyms: POST and BIOS. POST stands for Power On Self Test and it tells you whether your PC is working properly. BIOS, pronounced 'bye-oss', is short for Basic Input and Output System and it tells your PC what bits are inside it and what to do with them.

When you switch on your PC, though, you'll encounter a very small but very annoying problem: chances are, your keyboard isn't going to work. These days most keyboards come with USB plugs and most motherboards support USB keyboards. Unfortunately, that support is often turned off by default and you need to switch it on in the BIOS. To do that, you'll need a keyboard. Can you see where we're going here? Yep, you can't use your keyboard until you switch on your motherboard's USB keyboard support and to do that you need to use your keyboard. Which won't work.

There are two solutions. You can beg or borrow an old, non-USB keyboard, or you can use a USB to PS/2 adapter. Whichever option you use, you can switch on your motherboard's USB keyboard support and then get rid of the old keyboard or the adapter.

Our photo shows a standard USB to PS/2 adapter, which fits

If you've got a USB keyboard, you'll need one of these for a few minutes: it's a PS2 adapter that persuades your PC you have an old-style keyboard.

over the USB socket on your keyboard cable and enables you to plug it into the old-style PS/2 port on the back of the PC. If you're lucky, your USB keyboard will have come with such an adapter and you'll still have it; however if you're like us, you threw it out years ago. That means you'll have to nip to the supermarket to buy an ultra-cheap keyboard that includes the appropriate adapter.

Once you've installed the adapter or connected an old keyboard, it's time to switch on your PC and see what the POST has to say.

Beep codes

When you switch on your PC, you should hear a beep. What you're hearing is the result of the Power On Self Test, and if you

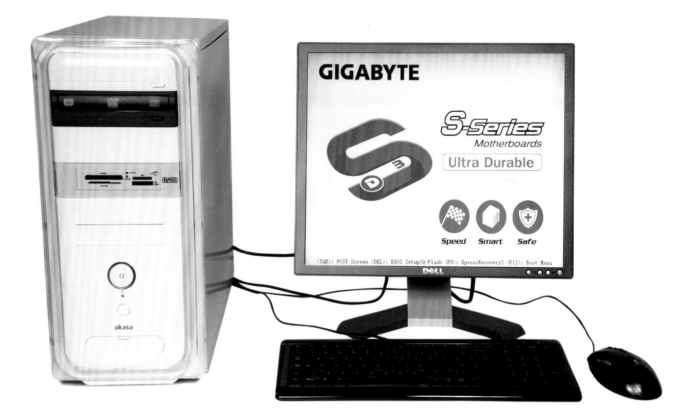

When you switch on your PC, you should see the splash screen. This is mainly an advert for the motherboard manufacturer, but it also tells you what keys to press if you want to access the BIOS setup.

have any major hardware problem you'll find out about it now. One beep is good, because it means that the POST hasn't found any problems. More than one beep isn't so good, because it means POST has found something bad.

The beep codes you hear will depend on which company created the BIOS, and you'll see their name on the screen that appears when you first power up your PC (provided, of course, that your video card is working). For example, if your motherboard uses a Phoenix BIOS and you hear one beep, then four beeps, then two beeps, POST is telling you that your memory isn't working; if you can't see anything on screen and you hear three beeps, then another three beeps, then four beeps, the motherboard can't find your video card. That might mean it isn't installed correctly or it could indicate that the video card is faulty. For advice on troubleshooting your PC, turn to p.146; for a full list of beep codes, turn to Appendix 3.

In most cases you'll hear a single, happy beep and the screen will display the 'splash page' that appears when you first boot your PC. This screen will tell you what key you need to press to enter the BIOS settings; in the case of our Gigabyte motherboard, we need to press <DEL> while the splash screen is displayed. If you don't press the appropriate key in time, don't worry; just reboot your PC and try again. After a few moments you should see your PC's BIOS and, while it looks quite scary, it's actually rather simple.

Changing BIOS settings

1

When the BIOS menu first appears you'll see some basic information on screen – typically, what keys you need to press to select menu options and edit their contents. What we're interested in, though, is the menu down the left hand side of the screen. Using the arrow keys, move the cursor until Standard Features is selected and then press Enter to go to that part of the BIOS menu.

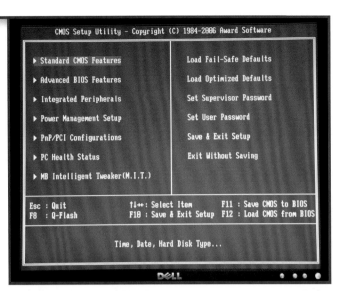

2

The Standard Features screen should now appear. There are two main things to check here: the system date and time; and the bits marked IDE Channel 0 Master and IDE Channel 1 Master. Your DVD drive and hard disk should appear in here; if they don't, then there's either a connection problem or one of the devices (or cables) is faulty. If everything's okay, just press ESC to return to the main BIOS menu.

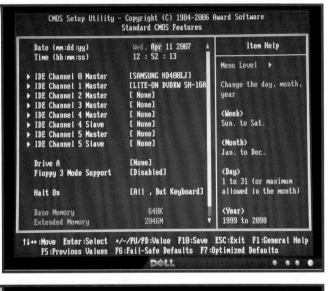

3

This time we want to go into the Advanced BIOS Features menu and adjust the boot order. The boot order is the order in which your PC looks at its various drives when you switch it on. For example, if you have a floppy disk drive as the first boot device, then your PC will look for an operating system on that when you switch it on. If it doesn't find it, you'll see an error message. With our PC we want to set our DVD drive as the first boot device and the hard disk as the second. There are several reasons for this. First, to install Windows we need to boot from the DVD drive; secondly, if we ever need to run a boot CD from our anti-virus software we need to boot it from the DVD drive before the PC turns to our hard disk. If your DVD drive isn't already the first boot device, change the order by pressing Enter to select the first boot device, using the arrow keys to select the DVD and then pressing Enter again to confirm the change. Press Esc when you've done this.

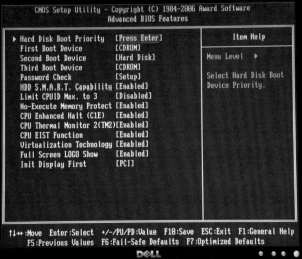

④

Now it's time to enable our USB keyboard. To do this, select Integrated Peripherals from the main menu. You should see two options – USB Keyboard and USB Mouse – and they're probably both set to 'Disabled'. We need to enable both options so we can use our USB keyboard and mouse with our PC.

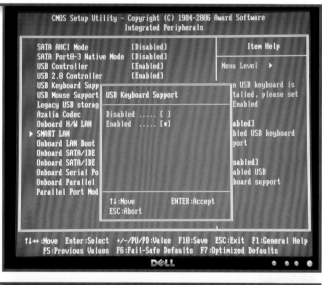

⑤

To enable USB support, use the arrow keys to select the appropriate option – in this case, USB Keyboard; some systems will call it Legacy USB Support or something similar – and press Enter. Now, use the arrow keys to select Enabled and press Enter again. That's the keyboard support turned on. Repeat the process for the USB Mouse option.

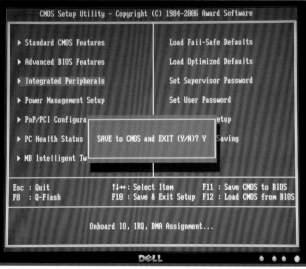

⑥

When you've turned on USB support, it's time to save your settings and exit. In our BIOS that means pressing the F10 key and selecting 'Yes' when the BIOS asks whether we really want to save and exit.

There's only one thing left to do now and that's to install the operating system.

PART **5** # Installing Windows Vista

Your lovingly assembled PC is ready to run, but you'll need to install an operating system before you can do anything useful with it. In this section, we'll discover which operating system to go for and how to get it up and running on your PC.

For our PC project we've chosen the OEM version of Windows Vista Home Premium, and there are a number of reasons for that decision. First and foremost, OEM (Original Equipment Manufacturer) copies are much cheaper than boxed copies – our OEM copy of Vista was around £60, while the retail version has an RRP of £219 – and, by going down the OEM route, Vista is really the only option: from early 2008 Microsoft will stop selling OEM versions of Windows XP, and at the time of writing they're already thin on the ground and cost the same as the newer, shinier, more desirable Windows Vista.

Why Home Premium? Of all the versions of Windows Vista, we think Home Premium offers the best trade-off between price and power. It offers all the important goodies such as the Windows Aero user interface, but it's much cheaper than the all-singing, all-dancing Ultimate edition. However, as we'll discover in this section, it's possible to experiment with Ultimate even when you've bought a lesser version.

Before you decide on an OEM version of Vista rather than a boxed, retail copy, it's important to know the limitations of an OEM licence. The most important such limitation is that OEM versions are only available to system builders and they're designed to be installed on and sold with a brand new PC. That means OEM licences aren't transferable. When you buy a boxed retail copy of Vista you can move it from one PC to another – it isn't easy, but you can do it – but when you go for the OEM version, the licence has to stay with the PC. We don't think that's a problem because our PC is designed to last for years.

The second issue with OEM versions of Vista is that you don't get any documentation and you don't get technical support. That's why it's so cheap, but if you'd prefer a nice glossy manual and a phone number you can call for help then it might be worth buying a standard retail version. If, as for us, price is more important, we'd recommend the OEM option every time.

Finally, you can't buy OEM versions in the shops. However, most reputable online dealers such as Dabs.com will happily sell them to you provided you're also buying PC hardware.

Whether you go for the OEM version or the retail version of Vista, the installation process is the same – so how do you install Vista on your brand new PC? Let's find out.

As you can see from the photograph, the OEM version of Windows Vista doesn't look very impressive: it's a dull cardboard box with lots of tiny text on it. You don't get a glossy manual or a nice box, but you do save more than £100 by going for the OEM version.

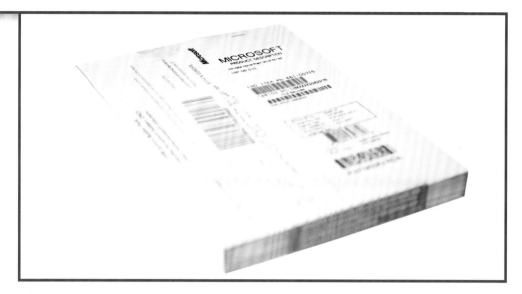

Inside the box you'll find a plastic DVD case. If your copy is legitimate, the DVD will be printed with a Microsoft hologram; if it isn't, don't go any further. Windows Vista uses a technology called Product Activation to spot dodgy copies, and after 30 days (or earlier if you try to activate Windows when you first run it) Microsoft will flip a kill switch that renders your copy of Vista unusable.

On the back of the DVD case, you'll see a label. Don't lose it: this contains your product key, and without it you won't be able to reinstall Windows at a later date. Once you've installed Vista it's a very good idea to affix the label to your PC's case, ideally in a place where it's easy to see if you need the product key in the future.

Installing Windows Vista is really very simple. Put the DVD in the drive, reboot your PC and after a bit of whirring the first installation screen will appear.

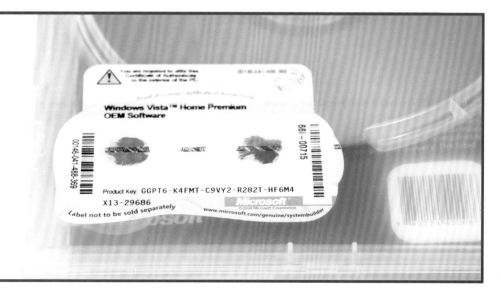

4

The first screen you'll see asks you to choose the language for your installation. Make sure that you choose the UK English and UK Keyboard options (assuming of course that you're in the UK and using a UK keyboard). If you select the US keyboard layout by mistake weird things will happen when you type, so for example instead of getting the @ symbol when you press the @ key, you'll get quotation marks instead.

5

This screen's straightforward enough: there's a great big button in the middle of the screen that says Install Now. Click it to continue.

6

The installer will now ask for your product key and there's also a tick box that says 'Activate Windows automatically when I'm online'. You can enter the key if you wish, but you don't need to do it right now – and if you don't, you can play with some interesting options, as we'll discover in the next screen.

7

Every Windows Vista DVD includes every version of Windows Vista, so even though we've bought the Home Premium version the DVD also includes the (rubbish) Home Basic Edition and the (excellent but expensive) Ultimate Edition. If you wish, you can use this screen to install a different version of Vista than the one you've paid for and you've got 30 days to play with it before you need to activate Windows and stick with the version you actually own (alternatively you can use AnyTime Upgrade at this point, which is a Windows feature that enables you to upgrade the version you've got to a nicer, more expensive version; naturally, this costs money).

You won't see this screen if you've entered your product key in the previous step. That's because the product key tells the installer which version of Windows you've actually paid for. If you're curious there's no reason why you shouldn't install the Ultimate Edition rather than the Home Premium edition, although there's absolutely no point in trying a cut-down version such as Home Basic.

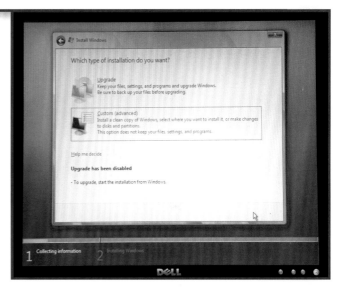

8

The next screen asks you to choose which kind of installation you want to perform, but in the case of OEM disks the choice is made for you and the 'upgrade' option is greyed out. That's because OEM versions are designed to be installed on a brand new PC that doesn't have an operating system to upgrade. The installer really, really wants you to click on the Advanced (Custom Install) option, and it would be impolite to disappoint it.

9

The installer will now ask where you want to install your copy of Windows Vista. Because we've installed a single, brand new hard disk there should be just one option here: unallocated space. That's the location we want to use, so click on Next to continue.

This would be a good time to make a cup of tea, because from now on the Windows Vista installer does everything automatically. Your PC will reboot a few times, the installer will show a few messages telling you how great Windows Vista is, and eventually the installation will finish. There are a few more steps we need to take before Vista is ready to use, but they're nice and quick.

10

When the installation is finished, you'll need to tell Windows Vista what to call you. This is because files are stored under user names and you can have several different people using the same computer. You'll also be asked to choose a password. You don't have to do this, but if your PC can be accessed by others it's a very good idea. Click on next to continue.

11

Now, the installer will ask you to give your computer a name. This is for networking and it's the label your PC will have when you're connecting to it from other networked PCs. You can't use spaces or unusual characters, so you'll need to choose something like JIM-PC here. You can also select a desktop background here; the list is fairly short, but there's a much bigger selection to choose from when you're actually using Vista. Once again, click Next to continue.

12

You'll now be presented with three different security options. 99% of the time the first option, Use Recommended Settings, is the one to go for. Unless you're already familiar with Windows Vista and plan to tweak its security yourself, stick with the recommended settings and then click on Next. The next screen will ask you to choose a location for your computer. Click on Home and then click Next.

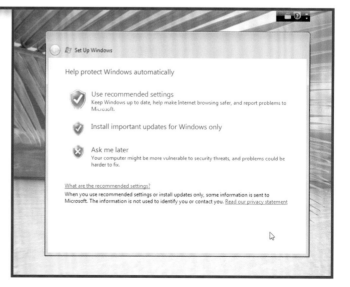

13

The next screen asks you to set the date and time, but they should already be correct – we set them in the BIOS a few minutes ago – so select the correct time zone, tick the 'automatically adjust clock' box and click on Next. You should now see the Thank You screen shown here. Click on the Start button and after a few seconds, the Windows Vista desktop will appear. You're finished!

Here's the result of all your hard work and the odd cut finger: a brand-new, home-made PC running Windows Vista. This would be a good time to give yourself a pat on the back or to do a happy dance.

Driving you crazy

One of the first things Windows does is scan your system to see what hardware's in it. Windows then attempts to install the necessary device drivers that enable it to communicate with that hardware. However, you're likely to encounter a few problems – especially if your hardware choices are unusual. The first problem is that Windows Vista might not know what your hardware is and the second problem is that, even if it does correctly identify your hardware, it might not have the appropriate drivers.

One solution to the problem is to use the various CDs that came with your PC components. There'll be a CD with your motherboard, another one with your graphics card and so on. However, one thing we've encountered fairly frequently is that the drivers on those disks are for Windows XP and not Windows Vista, which uses a completely different kind of driver technology. If that's the case with your hardware, you'll need to turn to the internet. For example, to get the most up-to-date drivers for our graphics card we had to visit the support section of the ATI website. Doing this is a major pain in the neck, but it's worth doing in order to get a stable system.

Most Windows Vista problems of the 'my screen isn't working properly', 'everything looks funny' and 'I can't select a high resolution' variety are the result of old or incorrect driver software. For example, if you can't persuade Windows to display the snazzy Aero Glass interface that's usually a driver fault. Installing up-to-date drivers and restarting your system usually solves the problem.

QUICK Q&A

Now what?

Windows Vista comes with some security software: Windows Defender, which tries to stop spyware from sneaking onto your system, and Windows Firewall, which blocks potentially malicious programs from connecting to your PC (if they're not yet on your system) or connecting to the internet (if they are on your system). However, we'd strongly recommend investing in a serious anti-virus program too. We've had good results with BitDefender AntiVirus and Panda AntiVirus programs, but there are lots to choose from.

When you first run Windows Vista, it's a very good idea to run Windows Update (Start > All Programs > Windows Update) to download the latest patches for your system.

Moving Vista from another PC

If the computer you're building is designed to replace another machine that's already running Windows Vista and you still have the installation disc, you can move that copy of Vista to your new computer provided that it isn't an OEM version (which is locked to the first machine you install it on – the licence terms prohibit you from moving it to a different PC). However, while the installation process is the same as with any other copy of Vista, once you've got your machine up and running you'll encounter an irritating problem.

When you try to activate Windows on your new machine, you'll get a message telling you that your product key has already been used. Don't despair, though: the activation screen gives you a phone number to call and if you're patient, you'll eventually be able to speak to someone who will deactivate the old product code (rendering the copy of Vista on your old PC redundant) and give you a brand new activation code for your new PC.

PART 5 Installing a sound card

If you are not content with integrated audio or if your motherboard lacks such capability, you'll want to install a sound card. This can be installed in any PCI expansion slot. First, though, revisit the BIOS menu and disable the onboard audio chip.

You can disable your motherboard's integrated audio chip in the BIOS menu. Do this before installing a sound card. If you leave the setting on Auto, the motherboard should recognise the presence of a new card and turn off integrated audio automatically – but there's no guarantee.

```
          CMOS Setup Utility - Copyright (C) 1984-2002 Award Software
                              Integrated Peripherals

   On-Chip Primary   PCI IDE  [Enabled ]                    Item Help
   On-Chip Secondary PCI IDE  [Enabled ]
   IDE1 Conductor Cable        [Auto     ]       Menu Level  ▶
   IDE2 Conductor Cable        [Auto     ]
   USB Controller              [Enabled ]        [Auto]
   USB Keyboard Support        [Disabled]        auto-detect AC97 Audio
   USB Mouse Support           [Disabled]
   AC97 Audio                  [Auto    ]        [Disabled]
   Onboard H/W LAN             [Enabled ]        disable AC97 Audio
   Onboard LAN Boot ROM        [Disabled]
   Onboard Serial Port 1       [3F8/IRQ4]
   Onboard Serial Port 2       [2F8/IRQ3]
   UART Mode Select            [Normal]
 x UR2 Duplex Mode             Half
   Onboard Parallel Port       [378/IRQ7]
   Parallel Port Mode          [SPP    ]
 x ECP Mode Use DMA            3
   Game Port Address           [201   ]
   Midi Port Address           [330   ]

 ↑↓←→:Move  Enter:Select  +/-/PU/PD:Value  F10:Save  ESC:Exit  F1:General Help
 F3:Language F5:Previous Values F6:Fail-Safe Defaults F7:Optimized Defaults
```

Turn off your computer, unplug it from the mains and take the usual antistatic precautions. Open the computer case and lay it on its side. Now familiarise yourself with the layout of the expansion card (i.e. read the manual), decide which PCI slot to use and remove the corresponding blanking plate from the case. Remove the card from its antistatic bag and carefully install it in the expansion slot. Be sure not to touch any components. Secure the card to the case chassis with the screw.

Now connect the audio cables from your CD/DVD drives – but see the note on p.137 first.

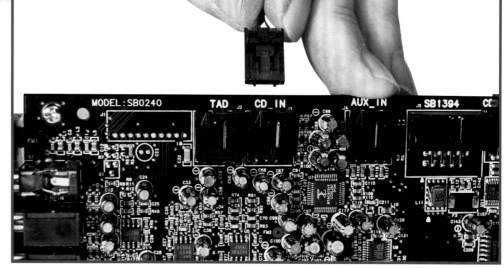

This card is supplied with an optional port bracket that supplies the computer with a MIDI/games port. It connects to the sound card by means of a cable. Note that a port bracket effectively blocks an expansion slot so you may prefer to live without one if slots are in short supply. With a small form factor case, you probably won't have the option to use a port bracket.

Remove a blanking plate and screw the port bracket into position next to the sound card. Finally, replace the computer covers, plug it in and fire it up. Windows will identify the new component and ask for a driver. Pop the supplied CD-ROM in the drive and follow the directions. You should also install any applications software shipped with the card and, of course, connect your speakers.

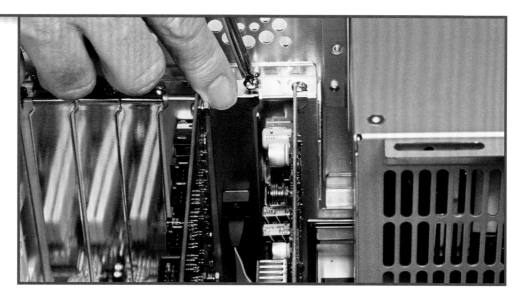

PART 5

Digital audio extraction

We mentioned earlier (p.63) that many drives support digital audio extraction (DAE). With speakers connected to the sound card, this is the time to find out.

First, establish that you can hear an audio CD when played in the CD/DVD drive. Then check that DAE has been enabled within Windows. In Windows XP, click Start, Control Panel, Performance & Maintenance and System. This launches the System Properties window. Look in the Hardware tab and click Device Manager. Here you will find a list of all the hardware devices in your computer. Click the little '+' sign next to DVD/CD-ROM drives and then double-click the drive in question. In the Properties tab, ensure that the 'Enable digital CD audio for this CD-ROM device' box is checked (ticked). If this option is greyed-out and unclickable, the drive does not support DAE and you'll definitely need to use an audio cable. Repeat with the DVD drive.

In Windows Vista, the easiest way to check everything's connected properly is to click Start > Windows Media Player and then click on the arrow below the Rip button. Choose More Options from the menu and a dialog box will appear. Click on the Devices tab, select your drive and then click on Properties. If everything's connected you should see 'Digital' selected in both the Playback and Rip sections.

Now turn off your computer, remove the covers and disconnect the audio cable from either the drive or the sound card. Reboot and try playing the CD again. If you still hear sound, you know that the drive supports DAE and you can remove the cable altogether.

Alternatively, of course, you can opt not to bother with internal audio cables in the first place and take a chance that DAE will work. That's what we do.

QUICK Q&A

How many PCI cards can I install?
As many as you have slots for on your motherboard. The PCI bus is natively 'Plug-and-Play', which means the computer can apportion system resources automatically and avoid hardware conflicts.

It's not such a huge deal, really, but Digital Audio Extraction lets you dispense with those fiddly internal sound cables. Anything that reduces the risk of cables snagging fans is welcome.

PART 5 **Loose ends**

You should now have a fully-functioning, home-built, better-than-off-the-shelf PC at your disposal. Congratulations – the hard work is done! If everything is behaving as it should, now is the time to consider further hardware installations to complete the picture.

There is one final, rather pressing matter to take care of, namely tidying your PC's interior. The trouble here is that there's no 'right' way to do it as such; it's really just a matter of bunching together surplus power cables and tucking them out of the way … somewhere. A free drive bay is fine. Keep dangling cables away from fans and other components, and ensure that, so far as possible, cables do not impede airflow through the case. Your computer case manufacturer may have included a few plastic cable ties, or else you can use your own. Avoid metal ties, even if coated in paper or plastic, as these could short-circuit the motherboard. Again, the benefits of a tall tower case with plenty of room are apparent, but even a mid- or mini-tower can be kept reasonably tidy.

In a mid-tower case such as this it's not always easy to clear away extraneous clutter. Just ensure that cables are kept well away from fans and check that airflow in and out of the case is not blocked. Here, the sound card's bracket cable is rather too close to the video card's heatsink.

A full-tower case is a cinch to keep tidy. This example is further helped by the use of round IDE/ATA cables instead of the usual flat ribbon cables and a side-mounted hard disk drive.

PART 5 Free software

You've blown the budget on your PC components, but don't despair: even if you've spent all your cash, you can still get seriously good software for your new PC.

Before you start looking for software, though, it's worth looking at Windows Vista itself. For example, the Home Premium edition we've chosen includes all of the following software:

- A decent web browser
- A good email client
- Security (firewall and anti-spyware)
- Photo organising and editing
- Windows Media Player for music, DVD and movies
- Media Center software that turns your PC into a complete entertainment centre
- Integrated CD and DVD burning
- Movie editing and DVD creation
- Scheduled file backup
- Games, including 3D chess

In some cases, you might also get software with the components you've bought. For example, our DVD drive came with a free copy of the excellent WinDVD playback software and some graphics cards come with free games. However, no matter what's inside Vista or what goodies you got with your PC components, the one thing you won't have is an Office suite.

Office suites take care of word processing, spreadsheets and so on. As with Windows Vista, you can get OEM versions of Microsoft Office 2007 at a reasonable price – at the time of writing, the OEM version of Office 2007 Home and Student Edition is around £75, compared to around £100 for the non-OEM edition – but, before you spend more money, it's a good idea to check out some of the alternatives. Thanks to Open Source software, it's possible to get a very good rival to Office for free.

The Home Premium and Ultimate editions of Windows Vista are stuffed with software, including DVD creation and even media center software.

The cheapest version of Microsoft Office 2007 is the Home and Student Edition, which costs around £75 in OEM form – but OpenOffice.org offers similar features for free.

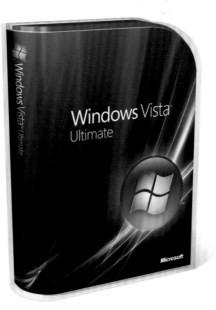

Introducing OpenOffice.org

OpenOffice.org is a very credible rival to Microsoft Office. It can read and write Office documents and it can do most of the things the various parts of Microsoft Office can do – but it's completely free. There's even a portable version that you can download and put on a USB pen drive, which means you can take the entire suite wherever you go and run it on any computer you like. If you've got broadband you can download it for free from **http://download.openoffice.org**, although we wouldn't recommend doing it on a dial-up modem connection: the Windows download is a mighty 106MB.

So what do you get for no money? There are six programs in the OpenOffice.org suite: Writer, for word processing; Impress, for presentations; Math, for mathematical calculations; Draw, for creating and editing images; Calc, for spreadsheet work; and Base, for managing databases. For most people Writer and Calc are where you'll spend most of your time.

OpenOffice.org looks very similar to Microsoft Office, so you don't need to worry about learning a whole new way of doing things. There are a few differences – things you'd expect to find under one menu appearing under another one, the odd button appearing in a different place and so on – but there's nothing too dramatic, and OpenOffice.org is a nice place to spend time in. It's also very powerful, and like Microsoft Office it's ideal for beginners and advanced users alike. However, as with most Office-a-likes don't be surprised if you encounter the odd problem

The open source package OpenOffice.org looks like Office and works like Office, but it won't cost you a penny.

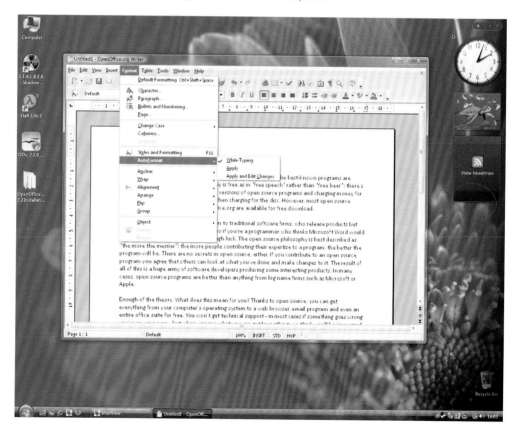

when you try to import very complicated files created in Word and Excel, and if presentation software is a key requirement then you might find the Impress program less impressive than rival products.

You can even make OpenOffice.org save in Microsoft Office-compatible file formats by default. To do this in Writer, for example, go to Tools > Options > Load/Save > General and choose the Microsoft Word 97/2000/XP option. From now on, every document you save in Writer will be in Microsoft Word format.

For most jobs, OpenOffice.org is very impressive but there is one key issue that you might want to consider. When you use most software there's a technical support department you can call; with OpenOffice.org, there isn't. You can find answers to most questions on the internet, but if you want the reassurance of knowing that you can telephone an expert when things go wrong, then OpenOffice isn't for you.

So how can OpenOffice.org give you a fully featured office suite for free? The reason is a philosophy called Open Source, which is responsible for producing lots of high-quality software and then giving it away for nothing. See the box 'free as a bird' on page 145 for more about the Open Source philosophy.

Other essentials

Anti-Virus software Although Windows Vista includes some security software – a firewall to block nasties, and a program called Windows Defender to spot malicious software – it doesn't have any anti-virus protection. Such software is essential when you're using the internet, but the good news is that you can get it for free.

There are several free anti-virus programs for Windows including AVG Anti-Virus (**http://free.grisoft.com**), AVAST Home Edition (**www.avast.com**) and the open source ClamWin (**www.clamwin.com**). Of the three, we like AVG and AVAST best, not least because at the time of writing ClamWin hadn't been updated to support Windows Vista. Both programs are free for non-commercial use, so if you use your PC for work then you'll need to pay for a commercial licence or look at a paid-for alternative product.

Multi-chat software Although Vista includes Windows Live Messenger, an excellent chat program, it's not a great deal of help If your friends or colleagues use a rival chat system. A multi-chat client, such as the excellent Trillian (**www.trillian.cc**), solves the problem by connecting to all the major chat networks and enabling you to communicate without running a different program for each network.

Online offices

The programs we've looked at so far all have one thing in common: to use them, you need to install them on your PC. However, a new breed of programs works in a very different way; instead of installing them you simply access them through your Web browser. You can use word processing software, spreadsheet software, email software,

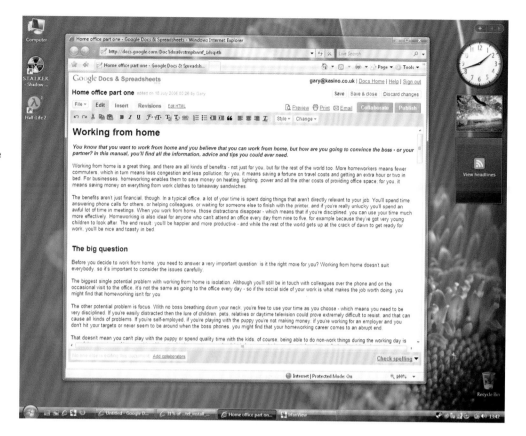

Google Docs & Spreadsheets provides basic word processing, spreadsheet and presentation features, and it all happens inside your Web browser.

calendar software ... if you can imagine it, there's probably a website that offers it. Even better, most such sites are free.

One of the best-known online suites is Google Docs & Spreadsheets (**http://docs.google.com**), which provides an excellent word processor, spreadsheet and, soon, a presentation package inside your web browser. The programs are all free (although there are paid-for versions that provide you with extra storage) and work very well, and while they're not as powerful as OpenOffice.org they're not supposed to be. If all you need to do is bash out the odd letter or analyse a few figures, Google Docs & Spreadsheets will do the job quite happily.

Google isn't the only firm offering free, online software. Lots of sites offer online word processing and spreadsheet software, and some of the computer industry's biggest names are getting in on the act too. For example Adobe, whose Photoshop is the king of image-editing software, has announced its plans for a free, cut-down version of Photoshop Elements that you'll be able to access from any web browser.

Provided you have a broadband connection – dial-up modem connections just aren't fast enough – there are several key benefits to web-based software. In most cases, traditional software costs a great deal of money, but most online applications are free. They're also updated immediately, so if they need a security fix or a bug fix you don't need to download it. Instead, the next time you access the program you'll automatically use an updated version. Finally, many online programs enable you to store documents online, which means you can work from anywhere you can get internet access instead of having to carry your documents around with you on a USB flash drive or a CD-R.

Google Reader LABS

Home
- **Home**
- **All items (100+)**
- Starred items
- Shared items
- Trends

Add subscription   Browse »

Show: updated - **all**   Refresh

- 160676
- Apple unofficial (100+)
- Applepeels (6)
- badscience (16)
- BatFlattery
- Bigmouth comments
- Bigmouth strikes again
- Daring Fireball (8)
- Darknet (6)
- Engadget (100+)
- Eurogamer (100+)
- Fafblog
- FreeMacWare.com (24)
- Idiot Toys (35)
- Lifehacker (100+)
- MetaFilter (100+)
- No Rock&Roll Fun (100+)
- Popbitch (100+)
- Scoble
- Squander comments (54)
- Squander Two
- the INQUIRER (100+)
- The Register (100+)
- Think Secret (16)
- UK Press Gazette (100+)
- UK Resistance (20)

Home

A look at what's new

New! We've made emailing items to friends even easier, with address auto-completion and HTML formatting. Click Email at the bottom of an item to try it out.

Daring Fireball (8)

An Anthropomorphized Brushed Metal Interface Theme Shows Up for the WWDC Preview Build of Mac OS X Leopard   Brushed Metal gets the news.

The High-Resolution 17-inch MacBook Pro   It's hard not to see the new high-resolution 17-inch MacBook Pro display as a few months ahead of its time.

Regarding iTunes Plus Metadata   Regarding complaints from 'privacy' advocates regarding the user-identifying metadata in DRM-free iTunes Plus tracks.

badscience (16)

The Mighty David Colquhoun   [Update: Letter from Provost below] Ben Goldacre Saturday June 9, 2007 The Guardian I've always said you'd get a lot more kids ...

Dr George Carlo responds to Andrew Goldacre   This post is only if you're not bored of the rather trying electrosensitivity lobby. Here is a letter which has popped up all ...

And science said atom bombs were safe too...   I'm in a dash, but I thought you deserved these two brave rebuttals of the peripheral criticisms that the ubiquitous ...

UK Resistance (20)

NOW THEY'VE UPSET JESUS!   We were slightly worried when we saw the headline "Church Calls for Resistance Ban" but it's nothing to do with us, oh no. It's ...

FORZA MOTORSPORT 2 - A REVIEW OF IT   We don't often bother with reviews as they're a lot of effort and words, plus most games are so boring they don't deserve any ...

A VERY STRANGE MOVING SEGA CHAIR   We got sent these photos of a huge SEGA chair. A man found it, bought it, restored it, loves it because it's weird and by SEGA ...

The latest messages from the Google Reader team

On the menu

via Official Google Reader Blog by Mihai Parparita on Jun 07, 2007
Sometimes we come across Reader-related things that are interesting enough that we'd like to post about them on our blog, ... See more »

Tips and tricks

Did you know that Google Reader has lots of useful keyboard shortcuts? Here are some of them:

- j/k: next/previous item
- n/p: scan down/up (list only)
- o/enter: expand/collapse (list only)

- s: star item
- <Shift> + s: share item
- v: view original
- m: mark item as read/unread

- r: refresh
- u: toggle full screen mode
- <Shift> + a: mark all as read

Click here to see the full list or press "?" to display it any time.

Although most web applications need an internet connection, a growing number can be used when you're not connected. Google Reader's newsreading program is one such package.

Web wobbles

For all the benefits of using web-based programs, there are plenty of negatives too:

It's only as fast as your internet connection Online applications depend on computers that may be hundreds or even thousands of miles away, and if the connections between you and those computers are congested then the performance of the program will deteriorate dramatically.

No connection, no software As you'd expect, you can't access online software if you can't get online – for example, you won't be able to use it if your ISP is having technical trouble.

It might not always be available We're big fans of online email systems such as Google Mail (**http://mail.google.com**), but we regularly encounter periods when the service isn't available – which means our email isn't available either. Other online services suffer from the same problems, so for example you might find that when you try to access the service to do something important it's 'temporarily unavailable' due to 'scheduled maintenance'.

It might not be very good Some online services – Google Mail, the 30boxes calendar system (**http://30boxes.com**) and so on –

are very good. However, some online services aren't. For example, ajaxWrite (**www.ajaxwrite.com**) was launched amid claims that 'for 90% of the people in the world, the need to buy Microsoft Word just vanished' but, in our experience, it's very basic, very slow, prone to crashing and it doesn't work in internet Explorer. It's a similar story with the online graphics program ajaxSketch (**www.ajaxsketch.com**), which has been described as an alternative to high-end graphics programs such as Adobe Illustrator. It's nothing of the sort.

There's no technical support With traditional software, there's usually a helpline you can call if you encounter trouble. With web-based software, there isn't.

If the site disappears, so does the software Google isn't likely to disappear any time soon, but what about the other online services? There are lots of me-too applications, for example, in the world of online word processors and spreadsheets there are dozens of sites offering essentially the same kinds of software. Inevitably some of those sites won't last, and if you choose one of the ones that doesn't last the course then there's always the risk that it'll disappear overnight and take the software – and your documents – with it.

It might not be free forever Most online applications are free, especially the ones labelled 'beta' (more of that in a moment). However, there's no way to predict whether a particular program will stay free forever, or whether it'll cost money at a later date. If you come to depend on a particular program and the developers decide to charge for it, you'll either have to pay up or spend lots of time moving your data to an alternative program.

It's usually in beta If – like most online applications we've seen – a program is labelled as a 'beta' or a 'preview', that means it isn't finished. 'Beta' is computer industry shorthand for 'help us find the bugs', and it's generally accepted that beta software might do strange things, crash your computer or even destroy your data. That's fine if you want to experiment with cutting-edge technology, but if you use beta software (whether it's online or on your computer) for business-critical tasks then you're taking a very big risk.

Web-based services are improving quickly and in a few years, they could well be a better option than traditional programs. For basic Office tasks they're well worth considering, but for heavyweight jobs we'd stick with traditional software, whether that's a big-name package such as Microsoft Office or an open source alternative such as OpenOffice.org.

TECHIE CORNER

Free as a bird

Open Source is all about free software. However, while most of the best-known programs are indeed free, the movement's philosophy is free as in 'free speech' rather than 'free beer': there's nothing to stop firms making their own versions of open source programs and charging money for them, or offering programs on CD and then charging for the disc. However, most open source software, such as the excellent OpenOffice.org, are available for free download.

The open source movement is a reaction to traditional software firms, who release products but prohibit you from fiddling with them – so if you're a programmer who thinks Microsoft Word would be better if you did some tweaking, tough luck. The open source philosophy is best described as 'the more the merrier': the more people contributing their expertise to a program, the better the program will be. There are no secrets in open source, either. If you contribute to an open source program, you agree that others can look at what you've done and make changes to it. The result of all of this is a huge army of software developers producing some interesting products. In many cases, open source programs are better than anything from big name firms such as Microsoft or Apple.

Enough of the theory. What does this mean for you? Thanks to open source, you can get everything from your computer's operating system to a web browser, email program and even an entire office suite for free. You won't get technical support – in most cases if something goes wrong you're on your own – but when you see what you can get for nothing, we think you'll be impressed.

Troubleshooting

Let's assume you've built your PC, turned it on for the first time ... and nothing happens. You can't get into BIOS, let alone install Windows. How and where do you begin to troubleshoot?

In fact, identifying a problem at this stage is very much easier than down the road when you've got a printer, scanner, webcam and goodness knows what other hardware attached; not to mention 57 software programs doing their utmost to interfere with one another, a real risk of viruses and perhaps a utility suite that does more harm than good. Your computer will never be so easy to diagnose and cure as it is right now.

Check the cables

The very first step is all too obvious but all too often overlooked: check that all external cables are securely connected in the correct places:

- ☐ The computer's PSU should be plugged into a mains wall socket (or power gangplank).

- ☐ So should the monitor.

- ☐ The mains electricity supply should be turned on at the wall.

- ☐ The monitor should be connected to the video card's VGA or DVI output.

- ☐ The keyboard should be connected to the computer's PS/2-style keyboard port (not to a USB port, unless USB support has already been enabled in BIOS, and not to the mouse port).

- ☐ The PSU should be set to the correct voltage and turned on.

Now turn on the monitor. A power indication LED on the monitor housing should illuminate and, hopefully, you'll see something on the screen. If not, re-read the monitor manual and double-check that you've correctly identified the on/off switch and are not busy fiddling with the brightness or contrast controls. It's not always obvious which switch is which. If the power light still does not come on, it sounds like the monitor itself may be at fault. Try changing the fuse in the cable. Ideally, test the monitor with another PC.

Internal inspection

Now turn on the PC itself. Press the large on/off switch on the front of the case, not the smaller reset switch. You should hear the whirring of internal fans and either a single or a sequence of beeps. But let's assume that all seems lifeless. Again, check/change the fuse in the PSU power cable. If this doesn't help, unplug all cables, including the monitor, take off the case covers and lay the computer on its side. Now systematically check every internal connection. Again, here's a quick checklist to tick off:

- [ ] The PSU should be connected to the motherboard with a large 24-pin plug and also, if appropriate, with ATX 12V and ATX Auxiliary cables.
- [ ] The heatsink fan should be plugged into a power socket on the motherboard.
- [ ] The case fans should be likewise connected.
- [ ] All drives should be connected to the appropriate sockets on the motherboard with ribbon cables.
- [ ] All drives should be connected to the PSU with power cables.
- [ ] The video card should be securely sited in its AGP or PCI Express slot.
- [ ] All other expansion cards should be likewise in place.
- [ ] Look for loose screws inside the case, lest one should be causing a short-circuit.
- [ ] If your motherboard has jumpers, check that they are correctly set.
- [ ] Check the front panel connections. If the case's on/off switch is disconnected from the motherboard, you won't be able to start the system.
- [ ] Are any cables snagging on fans?
- [ ] Double-check that Pin 1 positions on cables and drives are correctly matched (confession time: we initially got this wrong with the un-keyed floppy drive cable plug).
- [ ] Are the retention clips on the memory DIMMs fully closed?
- [ ] Does anything on the motherboard look obviously broken or damaged?

Disconnect each cable in turn and look for bent pins on the plugs and sockets. These can usually be straightened with small, pointy pliers and a steady hand. Reconnect everything, including the monitor and power cable, and turn the computer on once more. Leave the covers off to aid observation. Does it now burst into life as if by magic? Rather gallingly, unplugging and replacing a cable is sometimes all it takes to fix an elusive but strictly temporary glitch.

PSU problems

Look for an LED on the motherboard (check the manual for its location). This should illuminate whenever the PSU is connected to the mains power and turned on, even when the computer itself is off. The LED confirms that the motherboard is receiving power; if it stays dark, the PSU itself may be at fault.

When you turn on the computer, do the fans remain static? Does the CD drive disc tray refuse to open? Is all depressingly dead? This would confirm the PSU as the problem. Use an alternative power cable, perhaps borrowed from the monitor, just to be sure. If still nothing happens, remove and replace the PSU.

NEVER TRY TO OPEN OR REPAIR A PSU. Nor should you try running it while it's disconnected from the motherboard, as a PSU can only operate with a load.

Next steps

Let's assume that there is evidence of power flowing to the motherboard: the LED comes on and the heatsink and case fans spin. The PSU must be okay but there's still nothing on the monitor screen. Did you hear a beep as the computer powered up? This is a good thing. A sequence of beeps is generally a sign – a welcome sign, in fact – of specific, identifiable trouble. See the Power On Self Test (POST) section on p.149.

Check the keyboard. If anything is resting on the keys, remove it. This alone can cause a computer to pause. As the computer powers up, three lights on the keyboard should illuminate within the first few seconds. If they fail to do so, it's just possible that a dud keyboard is responsible for halting the entire system. Disconnect it and reboot the computer without a keyboard attached. If you now see a keyboard error message on the monitor screen where all was blank before, it looks like you need a new one. Connect an alternative keyboard to the computer and reboot again to confirm the diagnosis.

Another clue: if the computer partially boots but then stalls, check the memory count during the POST procedure. If the RAM total differs from the memory you installed, it looks like you have a DIMM problem to deal with. Remove, clean and replace each module. If that gets you nowhere, try booting with a single module in place, and experiment with each in turn. Check the motherboard manual for details here; a single module must usually be installed in a specific DIMM slot (usually DIMM1). If you can start the computer successfully at some point, you should be able to identify and exclude faulty modules. This isn't much help if you only have one module, of course.

Back to basics

Failing all of the above, disconnect all power and ribbon cables from the drives and the motherboard. Unplug and remove the video card and any other expansion cards, disconnect the case fans and leave only a single memory module in place. In short, reduce the system to a bare bones configuration where the only remaining connections are between the PSU and the motherboard: ATX power, ATA Auxiliary and ATX 12V. Do not

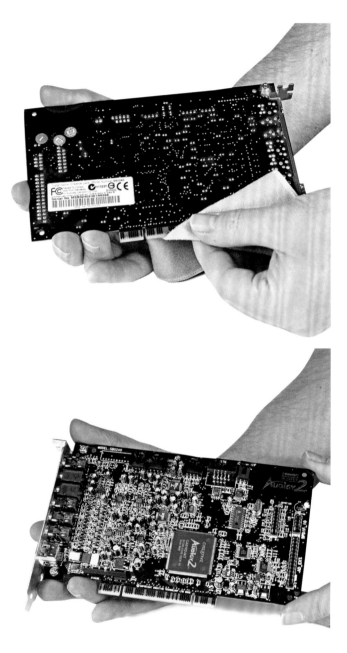

When handling expansion cards, be very careful not to touch either their onboard components or the lower gold connecting edge. With a card out of its slot, take the opportunity to clean its connecting edge with a lint-free cloth.

remove the heatsink or processor and leave all the front panel connections in place.

Now turn on the power once more. You should hear some diagnostic beeps from the BIOS. If so, see the following POST section and Appendix 3. If not, check the speaker connection.

If that doesn't resolve matters, turn off the computer, remove the power cable, and gradually, carefully, step-by-step, put it all back together again. Begin with the video card. Connect a monitor you know to be working and reboot the system. This will give you the added benefit of being able to read any onscreen error messages as you go along. If the screen stays blank, you know for sure that the video card is at fault. Replace it.

Reconnect a functioning keyboard next. Reboot and check that your computer gets past POST – i.e. that you can successfully enter the BIOS Setup routine. Now reconnect the floppy drive ribbon and power cables and reboot once more. Reinstall the hard disk drive next, followed by the CD and DVD drives. Every step of the way, reboot the computer and ensure that it doesn't hang or abort during POST. At some point, the computer may refuse to start – and right there you will have identified your problem. Alternatively, it may start normally all the way through and you may never find out what the original stumbling block was. No matter: either way, you have successfully solved your hardware hassles.

Power On Self Test (POST)

The very first thing a computer does when it starts is give itself a quick once-over to check that it still has a processor, memory and motherboard. If this POST procedure finds a serious problem, or 'fatal error', it is likely to throw a wobbly and halt the computer in its tracks. That's the assumption we have been working on in this section.

However, it also gives you two useful diagnostic clues (actually three, but hexadecimal checkpoint codes are beyond the scope of this book).

First, assuming that the video card and monitor are both working, you should see some onscreen error messages. These may be self-explanatory or relatively obscure, depending on the problem and the BIOS manufacturer, but should offer at least some help. A memory error would indicate that one or more of your modules is either faulty or not properly installed; a 'hard disk not found' message would most likely point to a loose connection or perhaps a faulty IDE/ATA cable.

Secondly, so long as the case speaker is connected, the motherboard will emit a series of POST-generated beeps. These can help you identify the specific component causing the problem.

We list some common beep code and error messages in Appendix 3.

POST is a low-key but essential routine that the computer runs through before launching Windows or any other operating system. Keep an eye out for error messages on the screen and an ear out for beep codes.

PART **6**

Appendices

Appendix 1 Silence is golden … well, copper
            and aluminium   **152**
Appendix 2 That's entertainment:
            making a media centre PC   **154**
Appendix 3 Beep and error codes   **158**
Appendix 4 Further resources   **163**
Appendix 5 Abbreviations and acronyms   **165**

PART ⑥ Appendix 1
Silence is golden ... well, copper and aluminium

If there is one thing the average desktop computer is not, it is quiet. Gallingly, the more high-powered you make it, the noisier it becomes. It all boils down to the cooling systems inside the case, i.e. a bunch of low-tech fans. There are fans in the PSU, fans built into the case, a fan on the processor heatsink, probably another on the Northbridge chip and yet another on the video card. Combined, they make a racket that's loud enough to be off-putting at best and to drown out music or game soundtracks at worst.

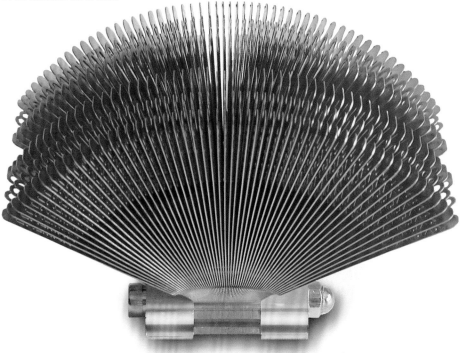

Freaky-looking it may be but this completely-silent Zalman 'Flower Cooler' can replace a boisterous CPU heatsink. All it needs is a really big, really quiet fan to supply it with fresh air.

However, there are some useful counter-measures available and here the DIY system builder can customise a computer to suit. For one, consider a passive heatsink for the processor, i.e. one without a powered fan. There are plenty of bizarre-looking but highly-effective heatsinks around that can keep the processor well within acceptable temperature limitations (under 75° Celsius for a Pentium 4).

Even chipset fans tend to be irritatingly intrusive, so you might care to remove the Northbridge heatsink and replace it with a silent fan-less alternative.

Most recent video cards also use fan-assisted heatsinks to cool the GPU. Here again it is often possible to replace the original with a silent version. Be careful, though: some of the latest video chips run so hot that a passive heatsink alone is not sufficient unless there is also a fan nearby to supply cool air.

There's little to do about a noisy PSU other than replace it with a quiet one – or, of course, to buy a quiet PSU in the first place. Check the specs and look for an acoustic noise level of about 30dB when the unit is running at 75% capacity.

Going further, you can even encase the hard disk drive in an acoustic enclosure and clad the interior of the case with sound-muffling panels.

Cooling caveats

Just a couple:

1. In smaller cases, the PSU is often located directly above the processor socket (as, in fact, in our project – see p.94). This generally rules out a passive heatsink because there simply isn't the necessary clearance over the processor. And even if you can squeeze one into the available space, don't forget that …

2. Even an elaborate super-effective passive heatsink needs some independent cooling. This is generally provided by a large, variable-speed ultra-quiet fan positioned directly above the heatsink and held in place with an angled bracket attached to the case. Again, this is not possible in most mid-tower cases.

In short, don't shell out for an inventive cooling solution unless you're sure your case can accommodate it. If you have an unobstructed view of the processor socket when the motherboard and PSU are both in place inside the case, you should be OK.

Consult Quiet PC for specialist advice and products, including the Zalman range of silent heatsinks (see Appendix 4).

If your chipset has a fan, consider replacing it with an efficient passive heatsink. So long as there is reasonable airflow inside the case, this will keep it cool and quiet.

If even the clicking of the hard disk drive drives you to distraction, encase your case in mufflers.

A silent copper-finned heatsink fitted to a video card cuts out one source of noise completely.

Appendix 2
That's entertainment:
making a media centre PC

All you need to know about domesticating a computer.

If your PC lives in a spare bedroom you might not be using its full potential: these days even the humblest PC is an entertainment powerhouse. So why not put it in the living room?

The computer you've built with the help of this book isn't just a powerful business and gaming machine. With the right software, a couple of components and a few simple tweaks it can be an all-singing, all-dancing multimedia marvel, so it's a shame to keep it tucked away in a spare bedroom or the study.

If like us you plumped for the Home Premium edition of Windows Vista, all the software you need is already sitting on your PC – and if you also installed a TV tuner card, all the hardware you need is there too.

Here's what your PC can do:

- It's a fully featured DVD player and you can connect your sound card to your stereo for stunning soundtracks.
- It's a digital jukebox that can store all your music and even your music videos, playing them through your TV or your hi-fi.
- It's a CD maker that you can use to burn your own compilation CDs.
- It's a movie marvel that can import and edit movies and then publish them to DVD.
- It's a showcase for your digital photos with special effects, videos and slideshows.

This is an off-the-shelf Media Center PC but you can just as easily build your own. Note the digital TV tuner card, which is all you need to receive Freeview channels.

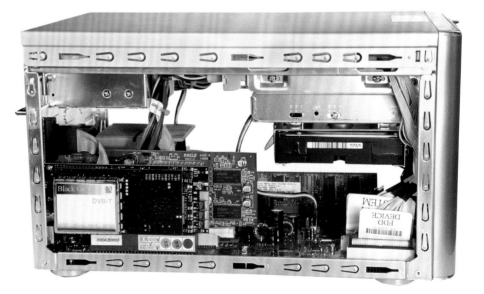

The Home Premium and Ultimate editions of Windows Vista include Media Center, which is designed to turn your PC into a multimedia marvel.

- It's a radio and an internet radio receiver.
- It's a digital video recorder that can record two channels at once – and it works with Freeview channels too.
- It's a door to a world of movie downloads, broadband TV and digital music.
- It's a home entertainment hub that can stream music to an Xbox 360.
- It's a games machine with graphics that consoles can only dream of.

Not bad for a humble PC, eh? However, to get the best from your PC's media features it's worth considering a few issues.

Think before you build it

A tower PC like the one we built in Part 3 might not be ideal for your living room, particularly if you're short of space or would prefer not to have a massive box in the corner. Noise is an issue too: a PC case with lots of fans can be very noisy and you don't want the quiet bits of a film spoiled by a PC that sounds like a jumbo jet. In many cases, you'd be better off with a small form factor PC like the one we built in Part 4, which is small enough to fit under your TV and quiet enough to do the job without spoiling your enjoyment.

Another option worth considering is a media centre case. Such cases are designed to blend in with the other equipment underneath your TV and, in addition to looking good, they're also designed to be quiet. In most cases you'll find that media centre cases follow the MicroATX standard, so there should be a wide selection of motherboards to choose from. Most of the major case manufacturers offer media centre cases and prices range from around £40 for a cheap and cheerful model to over £100 for something that looks like a really expensive hi-fi component.

Choose the right version of Vista

No matter which version of Vista you go for you'll get Windows Media Player, which can copy CDs and turn them into digital music files. It can also play DVDs, connect to online music shops and it's the software you need for most video-on-demand services such as the ones offered by the BBC and Channel 4. However, if you're serious about your media PC it's worth going for the Home Premium or Ultimate editions, as these include some extra features including better video editing, DVD publishing software and best of all, Media Center. Media Center has been designed to work on big screens such as TVs, and if you want to use your PC without leaving the sofa it's well worth having. Rather annoyingly, Microsoft couldn't be bothered changing the spelling from Center to Centre when it created the UK versions of Windows.

Get a good TV tuner

Every PC with a DVD drive can play DVD movies, but if you want to use your PC to watch or record television then you'll need to invest in a TV tuner like the one we installed in our first PC project. We plumped for Hauppauge's Nova-T-500, which offers several useful features. First, it's a twin-tuner card, so you can watch one programme while recording another one (or record two programmes simultaneously). Second, it supports Freeview, so you can get digital channels from your existing TV aerial without investing in a satellite dish or cable subscription. Thirdly, it's an FM radio receiver and also supports digital audio stations over Freeview. Fourthly, it includes a remote control so you can stay on the sofa. And finally, it's cheap: at the time of writing, Amazon is selling it for around £60.

A TV tuner really makes the most of Windows Vista's media centre software and it means your PC can replace your video recorder, your DVD player and your Freeview box. We'd strongly recommend investing in a Freeview-compatible card, because over the next few years all of the existing analogue TV transmitters will be switched off. By around 2011 – or several years before then, depending on where you live – the only way to receive TV broadcasts without a satellite or cable TV service will be via Freeview.

Make the right connections

If you're using your PC as a living room media centre you'll need to make a few connections, and you might need to invest in a few cables too. You'll need to connect your sound card outputs to your stereo (or just use a dedicated set of good quality PC speakers); you'll need to connect your TV tuner card to your TV aerial; and you'll need to connect your PC's video card to your TV. With modern flat screen TVs that's usually straightforward, as most of them have either VGA connectors or DVI connectors that accept standard VGA or DVI cables. With older TVs you'll need to use your video card's TV-out connector.

Cut the cables

Cables aren't always a good thing, especially if they're trailing across your carpet. In addition to a remote control, a wireless keyboard and mouse is a good investment. Early models had shockingly bad battery life but these days, wireless peripherals run for weeks and weeks on a single set of batteries – and you can hide them when you're not using them. A wireless keyboard comes in particularly handy if you want to play games or surf the internet on your big-screen TV but don't fancy sitting with your nose pressed up against it.

Another option: the home hub

Sticking your PC under the TV isn't the only way to take advantage of its entertainment possibilities. You could make it the hub of a home entertainment network too. Don't worry, it's much simpler and cheaper than it sounds!

The idea behind a home hub is that your PC stores all your stuff, but other devices can access it. For example, if you've already got an Xbox 360 in the living room you can get it to share data with your PC, which means your Xbox can access your PC's music, your movies and your digital photo collection. Once again Windows Vista includes the necessary software, so both Windows Media Player and the Windows Vista Media Center can stream software to other PCs or to your Xbox 360.

For that software to work, though, you'll need a network connection between your Xbox and your PC. A wireless network is the obvious answer, but there are two potential problems with that. The first one is cost – the Xbox 360 wireless adapter doesn't come with the console and it's a rather pricey £60; if you don't already have a wireless router you'll need to buy one of them too – and the second one is that wireless networks aren't perfect. If your house is full of brick walls and other solid structures or your Xbox is located quite far away from your wireless networking adapter, you might find that the wireless signal is weak and that the connection speed suffers as a result. That's not a problem for streaming photos, but a patchy signal can seriously affect the quality of streaming music and render video unwatchable.

Even if you've got a perfect wireless signal, existing wireless kit isn't fast enough for really high quality video streaming – but that doesn't mean you need to start drilling holes and running Ethernet network cables everywhere. Thanks to powerline networking you can get Ethernet speeds without Ethernet cables.

Powerline networking is enormously clever. Instead of using wireless signals, it uses your house's electricity circuit to deliver network data. All you need is two adapters: one for your PC or router and one for your Xbox or second PC. Connect each adapter to the appropriate equipment (the cables you need come in the box) and then it's just a matter of plugging each one into a spare wall socket and switching it on. After around 20 seconds the adapters will connect to one another and you'll have faster-than-wireless networking speeds without any drilling or cable clutter.

Early powerline equipment was fairly slow, but current models are as fast as normal Ethernet networks. Look for devices offering speeds of 85Mbps or higher and, as ever, take such speeds with a pinch of salt: in the real world, you'll probably get speeds of around one-quarter to one-half of the quoted maximums. That's still much faster than wireless, though, and it's probably much faster than your broadband connection too. Expect to pay around £100 for a high-speed kit that includes everything you need to connect two devices.

If that's whetted your appetite for entertainment and you'd like to know even more, including alternative hardware and software options, check out our *PC Home Entertainment Manual*.

If you've got an Xbox 360, you can stream music, movies and photos to it from your Windows Vista PC over a wired or wireless network.

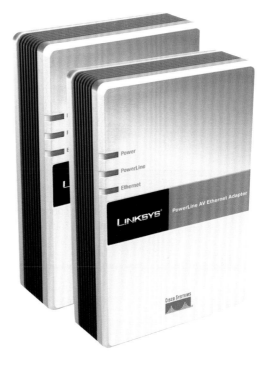

Powerline networking equipment transmits data via your house's existing electrical wiring. It's ideal for houses where wireless networks don't deliver.

PART ⑥ Appendix 3
Beep and error codes

As we discussed on p.94 and p.149, the motherboard –
or more precisely, the BIOS chip on the motherboard –
emits a sequence of beeps whenever it identifies a
problem that is serious enough to prevent the computer
from starting normally. If the BIOS does manage to get
the computer up and running, it can also generate
onscreen error messages that help you identify trouble
spots. Here we reprint the codes used by AMI and
Award, makers of two commonly used BIOS programs.

Phoenix, another major player, uses a rather more complicated
scheme that is beyond our scope here.

AMI BIOS beep codes

Number of Beeps	Problem	Action
1	Memory refresh timer error.	Remove each memory module, clean the connecting edge that plugs into the motherboard socket, and replace. If that doesn't work, try restarting with a single memory module and see if you can identify the culprit by a process of elimination. If you still get the error code, replace with known good modules.
2	Parity error.	As with 1 beep above.
3	Main memory read/write test error.	As with 1 beep above.
4	Motherboard timer not operational.	Either the motherboard is faulty or one of the expansion cards has a problem. Remove all cards except the video card and restart. If the motherboard still issues this beep code, it has a serious, probably fatal problem. If the beeps stop, replace the cards one at a time and restart each time. This should identify the guilty party.
5	Processor error.	As with 4 beeps above.
6	Keyboard controller BAT test error.	As with 4 beeps above.
7	General exception error.	As with 4 beeps above.
8	Display memory error.	The video card is missing, faulty or incorrectly installed. Remove, clean the connecting contacts and replace. If that doesn't work, try using a different video card. If you are using integrated video instead of a video card, the motherboard may be faulty.
9	ROM checksum error.	As with 4 beeps above.
10	CMOS shutdown register read/write error.	As with 4 beeps above.
11	Cache memory bad.	As with 4 beeps above.

AMIBIOS8 Checkpoint and Beep Code List version 1.2. Copyright of American Megatrends, Inc. Reprinted with permission.
All rights reserved.

AMI BIOS error codes Here are some examples of onscreen error messages:

Error	Action
Gate20 Error	The BIOS is unable to properly control the motherboard's Gate A20 function, which controls access of memory over 1MB. This may indicate a problem with the motherboard.
Multi-Bit ECC Error	This message will only occur on systems using ECC-enabled memory modules. ECC memory has the ability to correct single-bit errors that may occur from faulty memory modules. A multiple bit corruption of memory has occurred, and the ECC memory algorithm cannot correct it. This may indicate a defective memory module.
Parity Error	Fatal Memory Parity Error. System halts after displaying this message.
Boot Failure	This is a generic message indicating the BIOS could not boot from a particular device. This message is usually followed by other information concerning the device.
Invalid Boot Diskette	A diskette was found in the drive, but it is not configured as a bootable diskette.
Drive Not Ready	The BIOS was unable to access the drive because it indicated it was not ready for data transfer. This is often reported by drives when no media is present.
A: Drive Error	The BIOS attempted to configure the A: drive during POST, but was unable to properly configure the device. This may be because of a bad cable or faulty diskette drive.
Insert BOOT diskette in A:	The BIOS attempted to boot from the A: drive, but could not find a proper boot diskette.
Reboot and Select proper Boot device or Insert Boot Media in selected Boot device	BIOS could not find a bootable device in the system and/or removable media drive does not contain media.
NO ROM BASIC	This message occurs on some systems when no bootable device can be detected.
Primary Master Hard Disk Error	The IDE/ATAPI device configured as Primary Master could not be properly initialized by the BIOS. This message is typically displayed when the BIOS is trying to detect and configure IDE/ATAPI devices in POST.
Primary Slave Hard Disk Error	The IDE/ATAPI device configured as Primary Slave could not be properly initialized by the BIOS. This message is typically displayed when the BIOS is trying to detect and configure IDE/ATAPI devices in POST.
Secondary Master Hard Disk Error	The IDE/ATAPI device configured as Secondary Master could not be properly initialized by the BIOS. This message is typically displayed when the BIOS is trying to detect and configure IDE/ATAPI devices in POST.
Secondary Slave Hard Disk Error	The IDE/ATAPI device configured as Secondary Slave could not be properly initialized by the BIOS. This message is typically displayed when the BIOS is trying to detect and configure IDE/ATAPI devices in POST.

Error	Action
Primary Master Drive – ATAPI Incompatible	The IDE/ATAPI device configured as Primary Master failed an ATAPI compatibility test. This message is typically displayed when the BIOS is trying to detect and configure IDE/ATAPI devices in POST.
Primary Slave Drive – ATAPI Incompatible	The IDE/ATAPI device configured as Primary Slave failed an ATAPI compatibility test. This message is typically displayed when the BIOS is trying to detect and configure IDE/ATAPI devices in POST.
Secondary Master Drive – ATAPI Incompatible	The IDE/ATAPI device configured as Secondary Master failed an ATAPI compatibility test. This message is typically displayed when the BIOS is trying to detect and configure IDE/ATAPI devices in POST.
Secondary Slave Drive – ATAPI Incompatible	The IDE/ATAPI device configured as Secondary Slave failed an ATAPI compatibility test. This message is typically displayed when the BIOS is trying to detect and configure IDE/ATAPI devices in POST.
S.M.A.R.T. Capable but Command Failed	The BIOS tried to send a S.M.A.R.T. message to a hard disk, but the command transaction failed. This message can be reported by an ATAPI device using the S.M.A.R.T. error reporting standard. S.M.A.R.T. failure messages may indicate the need to replace the hard disk.
S.M.A.R.T. Command Failed	The BIOS tried to send a S.M.A.R.T. message to a hard disk, but the command transaction failed. This message can be reported by an ATAPI device using the S.M.A.R.T. error reporting standard. S.M.A.R.T. failure messages may indicate the need to replace the hard disk.
S.M.A.R.T. Status BAD, Backup and Replace	A S.M.A.R.T. capable hard disk sends this message when it detects an imminent failure. This message can be reported by an ATAPI device using the S.M.A.R.T. error reporting standard. S.M.A.R.T. failure messages may indicate the need to replace the hard disk.
S.M.A.R.T. Capable and Status BAD	A S.M.A.R.T. capable hard disk sends this message when it detects an imminent failure. This message can be reported by an ATAPI device using the S.M.A.R.T. error reporting standard. S.M.A.R.T. failure messages may indicate the need to replace the hard disk.
BootSector Write!!	The BIOS has detected software attempting to write to a drive's boot sector. This is flagged as possible virus activity. This message will only be displayed if Virus Detection is enabled in AMIBIOS Setup.
VIRUS: Continue (Y/N)?	If the BIOS detects possible virus activity, it will prompt the user. This message will only be displayed if Virus Detection is enabled in AMIBIOS Setup.
DMA-2 Error	Error initializing secondary DMA controller. This is a fatal error, often indicating a problem with system hardware.
DMA Controller Error	POST error while trying to initialize the DMA controller. This is a fatal error, often indicating a problem with system hardware.

AMI BIOS error codes continued:

Error	Action
CMOS Date/Time Not Set	The CMOS Date and/or Time are invalid. This error can be resolved by readjusting the system time in AMIBIOS Setup.
CMOS Battery Low	CMOS Battery is low. This message usually indicates that the CMOS battery needs to be replaced. It could also appear when the user intentionally discharges the CMOS battery.
CMOS Settings Wrong	CMOS settings are invalid. This error can be resolved by using AMIBIOS Setup.
CMOS Checksum Bad	CMOS contents failed the Checksum check. Indicates that the CMOS data has been changed by a program other than the BIOS or that the CMOS is not retaining its data due to malfunction. This error can typically be resolved by using AMIBIOS Setup.
Keyboard Error	Keyboard is not present or the hardware is not responding when the keyboard controller is initialized.
Keyboard/Interface Error	Keyboard Controller failure. This may indicate a problem with system hardware.
System Halted	The system has been halted. A reset or power cycle is required to reboot the machine. This message appears after a fatal error has been detected.

Award BIOS beep codes

Number of Beeps	Problem	Action
1 long beep followed by 2 short beeps	Video card problem	Remove the card, clean the connecting edge that plugs into the motherboard socket, and replace. If that doesn't work, try an alternative video card to establish whether the problem lies with the card or the AGP slot. If you are using integrated video instead of a video card, the motherboard may be faulty.
Any other beeps	Memory problem	Remove each memory module, clean the connecting edge that plugs into the motherboard socket, and replace. If that doesn't work, try restarting with a single memory module and see if you can identify the culprit by a process of elimination. If you still get the error code, replace with known good modules.

Award BIOS error codes
Here are the standard Award onscreen error messages:

Error	Action
BIOS ROM checksum error – System halted	The checksum of the BIOS code in the BIOS chip is incorrect, indicating the BIOS code may have become corrupt. Contact your system dealer to replace the BIOS.
CMOS battery failed	The CMOS battery is no longer functional. Contact your system dealer for a replacement battery.
CMOS checksum error – Defaults loaded	Checksum of CMOS is incorrect, so the system loads the default equipment configuration. A checksum error may indicate that CMOS has become corrupt. This error may have been caused by a weak battery. Check the battery and replace if necessary.
CPU at nnnn	Displays the running speed of the CPU.
Display switch is set incorrectly	The display switch on the motherboard can be set to either monochrome or colour. This message indicates the switch is set to a different setting from that indicated in Setup. Determine which setting is correct, and then either turn off the system and change the jumper, or enter Setup and change the VIDEO selection.
Press ESC to skip memory test	The user may press Esc to skip the full memory test.
Floppy disk(s) fail	Cannot find or initialize the floppy drive controller or the drive. Make sure the controller is installed correctly. If no floppy drives are installed, be sure the Diskette Drive selection in Setup is set to NONE or AUTO.
HARD DISK initializing. Please wait a moment.	Some hard drives require extra time to initialize.
HARD DISK INSTALL FAILURE	Cannot find or initialize the hard drive controller or the drive. Make sure the controller is installed correctly. If no hard drives are installed, be sure the Hard Drive selection in Setup is set to NONE.
Hard disk(s) diagnosis fail	The system may run specific disk diagnostic routines. This message appears if one or more hard disks return an error when the diagnostics run.
Keyboard error or no keyboard present	Cannot initialize the keyboard. Make sure the keyboard is attached correctly and no keys are pressed during POST. To purposely configure the system without a keyboard, set the error halt condition in Setup to HALT ON ALL, BUT KEYBOARD. The BIOS then ignores the missing keyboard during POST.
Keyboard is locked out – Unlock the key	This message usually indicates that one or more keys have been pressed during the keyboard tests. Be sure no objects are resting on the keyboard.
Memory Test	This message displays during a full memory test, counting down the memory areas being tested.
Memory test fail	If POST detects an error during memory testing, additional information appears giving specifics about the type and location of the memory error.
Override enabled – Defaults loaded	If the system cannot boot using the current CMOS configuration, the BIOS can override the current configuration with a set of BIOS defaults designed for the most stable, minimal-performance system operations.
Press TAB to show POST screen	System OEMs may replace the Phoenix Technologies' AwardBIOS POST display with their own proprietary display. Including this message in the OEM display permits the operator to switch between the OEM display and the default POST display.
Primary master hard disk fail	POST detects an error in the primary master IDE hard drive.
Primary slave hard disk fail	POST detects an error in the secondary master IDE hard drive.
Secondary master hard disk fail	POST detects an error in the primary slave IDE hard drive.
Secondary slave hard disk fail	POST detects an error in the secondary slave IDE hard drive.

PART **6**

Appendix 4
Further resources

Here are some useful links that will lead you to more detailed information on selected subjects.

High Street retailers

Maplin	www.maplin.co.uk
PC World	www.pcworld.co.uk

Web/mail order retailers

Dabs	www.dabs.com/uk
Bosse Computers	www.bossecomputers.com
Tekheads	www.tekheads.co.uk
Overclockers	www.overclockers.co.uk
Quiet PC	www.quietpc.com/uk

Computer fair contacts

Computer Fairs Information	www.computerfairs.co.uk
Northern Computer Markets	www.computermarkets.co.uk
Computer Markets Online	www.computermarketsonline.co.uk
The Show Guide	www.theshowguide.co.uk
All-Formats Computer Fairs	www.afm96.co.uk
The Best Event	www.bestevent.co.uk
Abacus Computer Fairs	www.fairs.co.uk

B-grade retailers

Morgan Computers	www.morgancomputers.co.uk
Dabs	www.dabs.com/uk/channels/Usedclearance
IT Dealers	www.itdealers.co.uk/catalog/index.php

High street and web retailers also sell-off B-grade stock from time to time; look for bargain bins, manager's specials and the like.

Consumer rights information

Trading Standards Institute	www.tradingstandards.gov.uk
Office of Fair Trading	www.oft.gov.uk

Processor manufacturers

Intel	www.intel.com
AMD	www.amd.com

Chipset information

Intel	www.intel.com
AMD	www.amd.com
ALi	www.ali.com.tw
VIA	www.via.com.tw
SiS	www.sis.com
Nvidia	www.nvidia.com

Intel and AMD also publish lists of motherboards that are compatible with their processors:

Intel	http://indigo.intel.com/mbsg/
AMD	http://snipurl.com/drwp

Memory information

Crucial Technology	http://support.crucial.com
Kingston Technology	www.kingston.com/ukroot
Rambus	www.rambus.com

Utilities

Intel Chipset Identification Utility
www.intel.com/support/chipsets/inf/chipsetid.htm

Sandra	www.sisoftware.co.uk
Ontrack JumperViewer	www.ontrack.com/jumperviewer

Audio technology

Dolby Labs	www.dolby.com
DTS	www.dtsonline.com
Steinberg	www.steinberg.net
THX	www.thx.com
DirectX	www.microsoft.com/windows/directx

Graphics technology

Nvidia	www.nvidia.com
ATI	www.ati.com
Matrox	www.matrox.com

CD/DVD technology

CD-Recordable FAQ	www.cdrfaq.org
DVD Demystified	www.dvddemystified.com
DVD+RW Alliance	www.dvdrw.com
DVD Forum	www.dvdforum.org

Hardware review sites

Tom's Hardware Guide	www.tomshardware.com
Motherboards.org	www.motherboards.org
ExtremeTech	www.extremetech.com
Anand Tech	www.anandtech.com
Digital-Daily	www.digital-daily.com

BIOS updates and information

Phoenix	www.phoenix.com
Award	www.unicore.com
AMI	www.megatrends.com
Bios-Drivers	www.bios-drivers.com

Manufacturers featured

Gigabyte	http://uk.giga-byte.com
AOpen	www.aopen.nl
Crucial Technology	www.crucial.com/uk/index.asp
Kingston technology	www.kingston.com/ukroot
Seagate	www.seagate.com
Mitsumi	www.mitsumi.de
Creative Labs	www.europe.creative.com
Lite-On	www.liteonit.com
Zalman	www.zalmanusa.com
Lian-Li	www.bossecomputers.com
US Robotics	www.usr-emea.com

Software featured

Windows Vista	www.microsoft.com
OpenOffice.org	www.openoffice.org
Google Docs & Spreadsheets	http://docs.google.com
AVAST antivirus	www.avast.com
AVG antivirus	http://free.grisoft.com
ClamWin AV	www.clamwin.com
Trillian	www.trillian.cc

All you ever wanted to know about ...

Form factors	www.formfactors.org
Serial ATA	www.serialata.org
Wireless networking	www.wi-fi.org
PCI Express	www.pcisig.com

PART **6** # Appendix 5
Abbreviations & acronyms

A handy list of some shorthand terms used throughout
this manual or that you might otherwise encounter.

2D/3D	Two-dimensional/three-dimensional	IDE	Integrated Drive Electronics
2x/4x, etc.	Double-speed/quadruple-speed, etc.	IEC	International Electrotechnical Commission
A3D	Aureal 3D	IEEE	Institute of Electrical and Electronic Engineers
AC '97	Audio Codec '97	ISA	Industry Standard Architecture
AGP	Accelerate Graphics Port	KB	Kilobyte
AMR	Audio Modem Riser	KHz	Kilohertz
ASIO	Audio Stream In/Out	LAN	Local Area Network
ATA	Advanced Technology Attachment	LED	Light-Emitting Diode
ATAPI	Advanced Technology Attachment Packet Interface	LGA	Land Grid Array
ATX	Advanced Technology Extended	MB	Megabyte
BIOS	Basic In/Out System	Mbps	Megabits per second
CD	Compact Disc	MCH	Memory Controller Hub
CD-DA	Compact Disc – Digital Audio	MHz	Megahertz
CD-R	Compact Disc – Recordable	MIDI	Musical Instrument Digital Interface
CD-ROM	Compact Disc – Read-Only Memory	MP3	Motion Picture Experts Group Audio Layer Three
CD-RW	Compact Disc – Rewriteable	MPEG	Motion Picture Experts Group
CMOS	Complementary Metal-Oxide Semiconductor	NIC	Network Interface Card
CNR	Communications and Networking Riser	NTFS	New Technology File System
CPU	Central Processing Unit	Pentium 4	Pentium 4
CRIMM	Continuity Rambus Inline Memory Module	PC	Personal Computer
DAE	Digital Audio Extraction	PCI	Peripheral Component Interconnect
dB	Decibel	PDA	Personal Digital Assistant
DDR-RAM	Double Data Rate – Random-Access Memory	PDF	Portable Document Format
DIMM	Dual Inline Memory Module	PnP	Plug-and-Play
DMA	Direct Memory Access	POST	Power On Self Test
DSL	Digital Subscriber Line	PS/2	Personal System/2
DTS	Digital Theatre Systems	PSU	Power Supply Unit
DVD	Digital Versatile Disc	RAID	Redundant Array of Independent Disks
DVD-RAM	Digital Versatile Disc – Random-Access Memory	RAM	Random-Access Memory
DVD-ROM	Digital Versatile Disc – Read-Only Memory	RIMM	Rambus Inline Memory Module
DVD-R/RW	Digital Versatile Disc – Recordable/Rewriteable	S.M.A.R.T.	Self-Monitoring Analysis and Reporting Technology
DVD+R/RW	Digital Versatile Disc – Recordable/Rewriteable	SATA	Serial Advanced Technology Attachment
DVI	Digital Visual Interface	SCSI	Small Computer Systems Interface
EAX	Environmental Audio Extensions	SD-RAM	Synchronous Dynamic – Random-Access Memory
FAQ	Frequently Asked Questions	SPDIF	Sony/Philips Digital Interface
FAT	File Allocation Table	TFT	Thin Film Transistor
FSB	Front Side Bus	THX	Tomlinson Holman Experiment
GB	Gigabyte	UPS	Uninterruptible Power Supply
GPU	Graphics Processing Unit	USB	Universal Serial Port
HDD	Hard Disk Drive	VGA	Video Graphics Array
HT	Hyper-Threading	Wi-Fi	Wireless Fidelity
I/O	Input/Output	ZIF	Zero Insertion Force
ICH	Integrated Controller Hub		

Index

2D/3D video card 59–60

Abacus Computer Fairs 163
abbreviations and acronyms 165
Accelerated Graphics Port see AGP
advantages of building your own PC 10
AGP (Accelerated Graphics Port) 26, 27, 29, 30, 31, 60, 62, 74, 161
ALi 163
All-Formats Computer Fairs 163
AMD 163
AMD chipset 28, 33, 42
AMD processor
    compared with Intel 33
    cooling 50, 75
    evolution 35–6
    installation 108–10
    memory 40, 41, 42
    memory controller 27, 39
    motherboard 28, 30
    PSU 50
    Sempron 30, 36–7, 72
    small form factor PC 74–5
AMI 164
AMI BIOS error codes 158–61
analogue monitor 61
    see also monitor
Anand Tech 164
antistatic mat 78, 80
antistatic wrist-strap 78, 80
antivirus software 142
AOpen 164
architecture, chipset 27
architecture, processor 35
Athlon processor see AMD processor
ATI 59, 62, 164
ATX form factor, case 45, 72, 73, 88, 155
ATX form factor, motherboard 25, 72, 73, 88
ATX PSU 48, 50
audio see sound card
AVAST antivirus software 164
AVG antivirus software 164
Award 164
Award BIOS beep codes 161–62

bandwidth
    AGP 26, 27
    boosting 41, 75
    bus 26, 27, 43
    disk drive 52
    memory 41, 42, 43
    network interface card (NIC) 68
    PCI 26, 27, 60
    PCI Express 26, 27, 60
    processor 26, 27
    sound card 58
    video card 27, 60
Basic Input/Output System see BIOS
beep (error) code in BIOS 158–62
Berg power connector 50
B-grade parts 15, 163

BIOS
    beep (error) code 158–62
    limitations 55
    S.M.A.R.T. support 54
    setup 126–7
    troubleshooting 149
    USB support 124, 127
Bios-Drivers 164
Bluetooth adapter 71
Blu-Ray 66
Bosse Computers 163
BTX form factor motherboard 25
building your own PC
    cost 10, 13, 15
    downside 11
    reasons for 6–7, 10
bus 26, 27, 43

cables, keeping tidy 138–9
cache
    hard disk drive 54
    memory 35, 37, 158
card reader 46, 70, 73, 75, 99
case
    dual-core desktop PC 73, 88–103
    features 47
    form factor 45–6, 72, 88, 155
    media centre PC 75, 108–19
    small form factor PC 75, 108–19
    style 19
    tidyness 138–9
CD drive see optical drive
CD-recordable FAQ 164
Celeron processor see Intel processor, Celeron
Central Processing Unit (CPU) see processor
chipset
    AMD 28, 33, 42
    architecture 27
    cooling 152–3
    driver 32
    Intel 28, 30–32, 33, 41
    motherboard components 26, 29
    Northbridge 22, 26, 27, 38, 152
    RAID 55
    selection 33, 72–3, 74
    Southbridge 23, 26, 27
    video card 59
ClamWin AV software 164
clock cycle 27, 41
clock speed 27, 33, 34, 35, 38, 42, 43, 72
CMOS error code 158, 161, 162
compatibility
    hardware–software 16–17
    motherboard and processor 24, 116
    motherboard and PSU 48–9
    motherboard and sound card 57
    recordable DVD 64
computer fair 15, 163
computer name 132
connector
    audio 58, 92, 93
    Berg 50
    chipset 33
    DVI 156
    fan 91, 123
    floppy disk drive 23, 27, 46

hard disk drive 52, 96–101
media centre 156
Molex 49, 50, 63
motherboard 24, 33, 52, 85, 91
network interface card (NIC) 68
power 49, 50, 95
SATA 49, 95, 99, 101
troubleshooting 147
USB, internal 93, 116
VGA 156
video card 26, 73
see also interface
consumer rights organisations 163
cooling
    'Flower Cooler' heatsink 152
    AMD processor 50, 75
    BTX form factor 25
    chipset 152–3
    fan 35, 38, 45, 47, 50, 85, 107, 118, 153
    heatsink 12, 35, 38, 39, 118, 152, 153
    installation 80–86, 110–112
    memory 39
    Northbridge chip 38, 152
    OEM packaging 12, 35, 38
    processor 12, 35, 152
    PSU 50
    retail packaging 12, 35, 38
    small form factor 75, 107, 110–112
    space 153
    troubleshooting 138, 147
    video card 59, 60, 73, 118–19, 138, 153
cost 10, 11, 13, 15, 29, 36, 37, 128, 141, 144
CPU (Central Processing Unit) see processor
Creative Labs 56, 75, 164
CrossFire technology 62
Crucial Technology 44, 73, 163, 164

Dabs 163
DAE see Digital Audio Extraction
DDR SD-RAM 30, 31, 40, 41, 42, 43, 44, 74, 75, 113
DDR2 memory 30, 31, 41, 42, 43, 44, 72, 73
desktop vs tower case 45–6
Digital Audio Extraction 137
digital monitor 61
    see also monitor
Digital Visual Interface (DVI) 61, 62, 156
Digital-Daily 164
DirectX see Microsoft
disk drive see floppy disk drive; hard disk drive; optical drive
Dolby Labs 57, 164
downside of building your own PC 11
driver, chipset 32
DTS 57, 164
Dual Double Data Rate RAM see DDR2
dual-channel memory 24, 28, 30, 31, 42, 43, 44, 74, 86, 113
dual-core desktop PC 73, 77–103
dual-core processor 33, 35, 36, 73
dual-monitor support 62
DVD demystified 164
DVD drive see optical drive
DVD Forum 164
DVD+RW Alliance 164
DVI see Digital Visual Interface

eBay 13, 163
error (beep) code in BIOS 158–62
expandability 7, 25
expansion card
    blanking plate 47
    FireWire (IEEE-1394) 69
    IDE/ATA interface 71
    installation 102, 118–19, 135–6
    integrated sound, compared with 32, 57–8
    integrated video, compared with 29, 32, 60
    PCI 26, 69, 71
    RAID adapter 55
    second-hand 12
    sound 135–6
    video 29
    wireless networking 69, 75
ExtremeTech 164

fair, computer 15, 163
fan 35, 38, 45, 47, 50, 85, 91, 107, 118, 153
FireWire (IEEE-1394) card 69
flexibility 10, 19, 70
floppy disk drive
    BIOS setup 126
    connector 23, 27, 46
    installation 99, 116, 126
    media card reader 70, 73
    media centre PC 74, 75
    power connector (Berg) 50
    small form factor PC 74, 75
    troubleshooting 147, 149, 162
'Flower Cooler' heatsink 152
form factor, case 45, 72, 88, 155, 164
form factor, motherboard 25, 72, 73, 88, 164
free software 140–45
front panel port 23, 92, 147, 149
front side bus (FSB) 26, 27, 31, 35, 43, 72

gaming
    controller 57
    processor 17, 33, 37, 40
    sound card 56–7
    standards 61
    video card 17, 61
Gigabyte (manufacturer) 44, 73, 125, 164
Google Docs & Spreadsheets 164
GPU see graphics processing unit (GPU)
graphics card see video card
graphics processing unit (GPU) 59

hard disk drive
    BIOS setup 126
    IDE/ATA interface 23, 24, 26, 27, 32, 49, 52–3
    installation 98, 114–5
    specification 51–5
    troubleshooting 149, 159, 160, 162
hardware–software compatibility 16–17
HD-DVD 66
headphones 70
heatsink 12, 35, 38, 39, 118, 152–3
    see also cooling
home entertainment PC see media centre PC
home hub 157
HyperTransport bus 74

IDE/ATA interface 23, 24, 26, 27, 32, 49, 52–3, 63
IEEE-1394 (FireWire) card 69
installation
    floppy disk drive 99, 116, 126
    heatsink 80–86, 110–112
    video card 102–3, 118–9, 147, 148, 149
Integrated Drive Electronics see IDE drive
integrated LAN 32
integrated sound 32, 57–8
integrated video 29, 32, 60
Intel 163
Intel processor
    Celeron 36–7
    chipset 28, 30–32, 33, 41
    clock speed 35
    compared with AMD 33
    cost 34–5
    dual-core desktop PC 73
    evolution 35–6
    installation 80–83
interface
    FireWire (IEEE-1394) 69
    hard disk drive 23, 24, 26, 27, 32, 49, 52–3
    optical drive 63
    video card 60
    wireless networking 69
    see also connector
IT Dealers 163

joystick 16, 70
jumper 53, 63, 79, 96, 114, 147

keyboard, USB support for 124, 127
Kingston Technology 75, 163, 164

legacy-free motherboard 23
Level 2 cache memory 35, 37
Lian-Li 46, 164
light for working 79
limitations of BIOS 55
Lite-On 75, 164

mail order 14
manufacturers 163–4
Maplin 36, 163
master and slave drive 53, 96
mat, antistatic 78, 80
Matrox 59, 62, 164
media card reader 46, 70, 73, 75, 99
media centre PC 140, 154–7
    see also small form factor PC
memory (RAM)
    bandwidth 41, 42, 43
    cooling 39
    DDR SD-RAM 30, 31, 40, 41, 42, 43, 44, 74, 75, 113
    DDR2 30, 31, 41, 42, 43, 44, 72, 73
    DIMMs 40, 44, 113, 148
    dual-channel 24, 28, 30, 31, 42, 43, 44, 74, 86, 113
    installation 86–7, 113
    requirements 17, 39–45

SD-RAM 15, 42
    selection 44
Memory Adviser 44
memory cache 35, 37, 158
microphone 22, 29, 70, 92
Microsoft 12, 16, 40, 66, 128, 129, 140–2, 145, 164
Mini-ITX form factor motherboard 25
Mitsumi 75, 164
modem 67, 122
Molex drive connector 49, 50, 63
monitor 59, 61, 62, 122–3, 146, 148, 149
    see also video card
Morgan Computers 13, 163
motherboard
    chipset 26, 29
    connector 24, 33, 52, 85, 91
    cost 11, 29
    FireWire (IEEE-1394) interface 69
    form factor 25, 72, 73, 88
    IDE/ATA interface 24, 26, 30, 32, 52
    installation 88–93, 106–8
    integrated LAN 32
    integrated sound 32, 57–8
    integrated video 29, 32, 60
    legacy-free 23
    power connector 50
    processor support 30
    selection 22–33
    socket 22–4, 28, 30, 35, 42, 49
    tray 47, 80, 88
Motherboards.org 164
movies see sound card; video editing
muffler 153
multi-chat software 142
multimedia, integrated 29, 32, 57–8, 60
multiple-monitor support 59, 62
music see sound card

Nano-ITX form factor motherboard 25
network interface card (NIC) 68
networking Xbox and PC 157
NIC see network interface card
noise level 38, 48, 50, 152–3, 155
Northbridge chip 22, 26, 27, 38, 152
Northern Computer Markets 163
Nvidia 59, 62, 74, 163, 164

OEM packaging 12, 35, 38
Office of Fair Trading 163
online software 142–4
open source software 145
OpenOffice.org 141–2, 164
optical drive
    DVD drive 64, 66
    IDE/ATA interface 24, 26, 52, 63
    installation 96–7, 117
    master and slave 96
    Molex connector 50
    recordable DVD 64
    SATA interfaces 26, 63
    speed 65
    technology 63–6
Overclockers 163

parts, where to buy 12–13, 14, 15, 36, 163
passive heatsink see heatsink
PC World 163

PCI bus 26, 27, 29, 30, 31, 60
PCI Express bus 11, 13, 22, 23, 24, 26, 27, 29, 30, 31, 58, 60, 72, 73, 164
Pentium processor see Intel processor
Peripheral Component Interconnect see PCI; PCI Express
Phoenix 125, 158, 161–2, 164
pliers 79
POST (power on self test) 124–5, 148–9
power connector 49, 50, 95
power on self test see POST
power supply unit (PSU)
    air vent 13
    AMD processor 50
    ATX form factor 48, 50
    case 45, 47
    compatibility with motherboard 48–9
    cooling 50, 153
    device connector 49, 50, 96, 99, 103
    installation 94–5, 99
    noise 48, 50, 153, 155
    power rating 50
    SATA connector 49
    testing 122–3
    troubleshooting 146, 147, 148
powerline networking 157
processor
    architecture 35
    bandwidth 26, 27
    clock cycle 27, 41
    clock speed 33, 34, 35, 38, 72
    compatibility with motherboard 24, 116
    cooling 12, 35, 152
    cost 34–5, 37
    dual-core processor 33, 35, 36, 73
    front side bus (FSB) 26, 27, 31, 35, 43, 72
    HyperTransport bus 74
    installation 80–83, 108–10
    Level 2 cache memory 35, 37, 75
    OEM packaging 12, 35, 38
    power connector 50
    retail packaging 12, 35, 38
    selection 33, 34–7
    speed 35
    video editing 17–18
    see also AMD processor; Intel processor
PSU see power supply unit (PSU)

Quiet PC 163

RAID (Redundant Array of Independent Disks) 55
RAM see memory (RAM)
Rambus 40, 163
reasons for building your own PC 6–7, 10
recordable DVD 64
recording see sound card
resources, web 163–4
retail packaging 12, 35, 38
retailers 15, 163

SATA bus
    bandwidth 27, 52
    chipset 26, 30
    connector 32, 49, 95, 96, 99, 100, 101
    data transfer rate 52–3
    expansion card 71
    information about 164
    optical drive 63
    power connector 49, 50
    PSU 49, 50

Scalable Link Interface (SLI) technology 62
screen see monitor
screwdriver 79
SCSI 53
SD-RAM (Synchronous Dynamic RAM) 15, 42
Seagate 75, 164
second-hand part 12–13
selection of chipset 33, 72–3, 74
Sempron processor see AMD processor, Sempron
Serial Advanced Technology Attachment see SATA drive
setup, BIOS 126–7
SFF PC see small form factor PC
shopping see OEM packaging; parts, where to buy; retail packaging
Shuttle see small form factor PC
SiS 163
slave and master drive 53, 96
Small Computer Systems Interface see SCSI
small form factor PC 74, 75, 104–19
S.M.A.R.T. disk drive support 54, 160
software 11, 13, 16–17, 128, 140–45, 164
sound card
    audio driver 58
    bandwidth 58
    compatibility with motherboard 57
    connector 58, 92, 93
    gaming 56–7
    installation 136
    vs integrated sound 32, 57–8
    MIDI port 57
    music 56
    recording 57
    THX 56, 164
    watching movies 57
Southbridge chipset 23, 26, 27
space for cooling device 153
speed
    optical drive 65
    processor 35
spindle speed, hard disk drive 54
Steinberg 164
style of case 19
Super I/O chip 27

technology information 164
Tekheads 163
TFT screen see monitor
The Best Event 163
The Show Guide 163
THX 56, 164
Tom's Hardware Guide 164
tools required 78–9
tower vs desktop case 45–6
Trading Standards Institute 163
tray, motherboard 47, 80, 88
Trillian 164
troubleshooting 88, 138, 146–9, 158–62
TV tuner 62
TV-out 62

Uninterruptible Power Supply (UPS) 71
Universal Serial Bus see USB
UPS (Uninterruptible Power Supply) 71
US Robotics 75, 164
USB 93, 116, 124, 127
used parts 12–13

VDU see monitor
VGA connector 156

VGA video card 62
VIA 25, 163
video card 2D/3D 59–60
    AGP 60
    analogue monitor 61
    bandwidth 27, 60
    chipset 59
    connector 26, 73
    cooling 59, 60, 73, 118–19, 138, 152, 153
    CrossFire technology 62
    dual-core desktop PC 73
    dual-monitor support 62
    DVI 61–2
    gaming 17, 62
    graphics processing unit (GPU) 59
    installation 102–3, 118–9
    vs integrated video 29, 32, 60
    interface 60
    media centre PC 75–6
    PCI 29, 30, 31
    SLI technology 62
    small form factor PC 75–6
    troubleshooting 147, 148, 149
    TV tuner 62
    TV-out 62
    VGA 62
video editing 17–18, 37, 40
video in 62
Vista see Windows Vista

web resources 163–4
web vendors 14, 163
web-based software 142–4
Wi-Fi see wireless networking
Windows Vista
    digital audio extraction 137
    drivers 134
    dual-core support 36
    installation 128–34
    media centre PC 154–7
    reactivation 134
    software included 140
    system requirements 13, 40
    web resource 164
wireless networking 69, 75, 164
working environment 78–9
wrist-strap, antistatic 78, 80
Xbox and PC, networking 157

Zalman heatsink 152, 153, 164

Authors	**Kyle MacRae and Gary Marshall**
Copy Editor	**Shena Deuchars**
Photography	**Iain McLean**
Front cover illustration	**Digital Progression**
Page build	**James Robertson**
Index	**Shena Deuchars**
Project Manager	**Louise McIntyre**